To Ron
7/15/92

Bob Dean

GOD'S BIG LITTLE WORDS

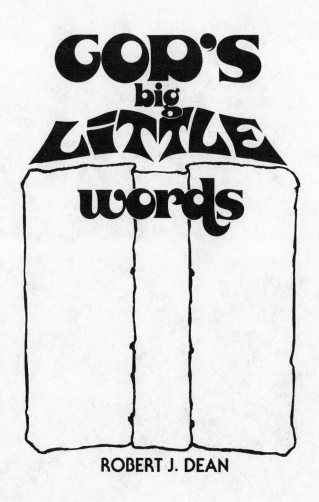

GOD'S big LITTLE words

ROBERT J. DEAN

BROADMAN PRESS • NASHVILLE, TENNESSEE

© Copyright 1975 · Broadman Press
All rights reserved
4281-24
ISBN: 0-8054-8124-9

Dewey Decimal Classification: 242
Library of Congress Catalog Card Number: 74-82583
Printed in the United States of America

Contents

Contents

Introduction

In Marc Connelly's play *Green Pastures* the opening scene is set in a children's Sunday School class of a rural black church. The preacher, Mr. Deshee, is giving a kind of running account of the early chapters of Genesis. He concludes by asking his group of boys and girls how they think they are going to like the Bible. One girl, Myrtle by name, gives this response: "I think it's jest wonderful, Mr. Deshee. I cain't understand any of it." [1]

Myrtle's evaluation of the Bible is shared by many, although they are seldom as honest as she was. Many people say good things about the Bible, but they seldom read it. Often this is at least partly because they consider it a difficult and obscure book.

Another segment of the population considers the Bible not only obscure but also irrelevant. These people do not say good things about the Bible. If they say anything about it, they criticize it as outdated and unimportant. They assume that the Bible is filled with meaningless theological jargon which has nothing at all to do with the problems of modern life.

However, within recent years many people have been rediscovering the Bible. Millions of people are reading and studying the Bible. Among these are some who formerly either ignored or criticized it.

A number of factors have contributed to this revival of interest in the Bible. One of these factors has been the availability of modern-speech translations and paraphrases. These have been keys to unlock the meaning of the Bible. People have discovered that the Bible is not written in some unknown code of puzzling theological language.

Perhaps the greatest discovery made by those reading the Bible for the first time is how life-centered the Bible is. Although the books of the Bible were written centuries ago, the message is amazingly contemporary. The Bible writers zeroed in on the deepest interests and needs of people.

One of the prevailing assumptions of recent years has been that modern man represents a generation that has "come of age." This generation is supposed to have reached a level of maturity and sophistication that sets us apart from our forefathers. According to this view, we no longer need many of the religious "props" with which our forefathers undergirded their lives. This arrogant presupposition has been the conscious or unconscious assumption of multitudes in our day.

Those who have rediscovered the Bible have reason to question this assumption, for this ancient Book speaks about the very things that people today are seeking—life, love, hope, joy, peace. These were the goals and aspirations of people in Bible times; these are also the goals and aspirations of people today. Listen to what you say and what others say. Read what people are writing about. How often do these words appear? People are talking and writing about their quest for life, love, hope, joy, and peace. And these are the very words that stand out when you read the Bible!

The really *big* words in the Bible, as in modern life, are the *little* words like *life, love, hope, joy,* and *peace.* When we speak of "big" words, we usually think of long words. The Bible has some of these—words like *justification* and *propitiation.* However, the really "big" words are not the long words but the key words. And the key words are words like *life, love, hope, joy,* and *peace.*

Look up one of these words in a Bible concordance, and count the number of times the word is used. Look up the references, and see how the word is used. You will find that these "big little" words are used repeatedly and at all levels of biblical revelation.

You also will find that these words carry the basic message of the Bible. These words do not occur primarily in obscure passages on the periphery of the Bible's real message. These words occur right at the heart of what the Bible has to say. The message of the Bible has to do with life, love, hope, joy, and peace. These are the realities that God seeks to impart to us.

A study of what the Bible says about life, love, hope, joy, and peace is proper for anyone interested in these realities. And who isn't? We are interested for our own sake and for the sake of others. If Christians want to communicate the good news today, we can best do so in terms of what people today are seeking. People today want life and love. They are looking for hope and joy. They are desperately seeking peace. Christians can say: "Look, these are the very things about which the Bible speaks. This is what the Christian good news is all about!"

This book is an attempt to show as clearly as possible what the Bible says about GOD'S BIG LITTLE WORDS. This book is not a technical study of the Hebrew and Greek words involved. Such a study is necessary background for any serious attempt to write about what the Bible means by the various words translated *life, love, hope, joy,* and *peace.* However, the results of such a technical study and not the details of it are mentioned in this book. Hebrew and Greek words are touched on but only where reference to them seems necessary for clarity and understanding. Those who want to read a technical and detailed study of the Greek words should consult the *Theological Dictionary of the New Testament.* [2]

Most technical word studies major on the distinctive shades of meaning of each word in the various strata of biblical revelation. For example, a Greek word might be studied as it is found in the Greek translation of the Old Testament, the Synoptic Gospels, Paul's writings, John's writings, and so forth. This is a necessary and legitimate step in such word studies.

However, GOD'S BIG LITTLE WORDS seeks to carry the study one step further: this book seeks to distill what are the major biblical teachings about each word as the word relates to life today. This approach does not ignore the distinctive contributions of each stage of biblical revelation; rather it seeks to build on these. The chapter titles and subheads in this book reflect overall aspects of what the Bible says about each word being studied; and these are stated in terms of life today.

---

[1] Marc Connelly, *Green Pastures* (New York: Rinehart and Company, Inc., 1958), p. 4.

[2] *Theological Dictionary of the New Testament.* Edited by Gerhard Kittel, translator and editor Geoffrey W. Bromiley (Grand Rapids: Wm. B. Eerdmans Publishing Co., 1963).

li**f**e —our most precious possession 1

Have you ever noticed how often the words *life* and *live* are used in television commercials? Everything from soft drinks to summer vacations, from beer to breakfast cereal is tied in with the built-in interest in life and living. The advertisers seek to identify a certain product with the basic human drive to live a rich, full life.

The commercial for one brand of cola, for example, is built around the word "live" which is shouted at top volume in a full crescendo of sound. A commercial for one kind of beer even sets forth a sort of philosophy of life: since each of us goes around only once in life, each person should live life with gusto.

Everyone is interested in life and living; however not everyone is optimistic about its prospects. The rigors and frustrations of life produce in some people a cynicism that is the opposite extreme of the shallow optimism of the television commercials. Shakespeare put these haunting words into the mouth of Macbeth:

> Life's but a walking shadow, a poor player
> That struts and frets his hour upon the stage
> And then is heard no more; it is a tale
> Told by an idiot, full of sound and fury,
> Signifying nothing.

Macbeth's gloomy analysis of life is echoed by many in our modern age. A few years ago a college paper offered a prize for the best definition of life. Here are some of the entries that won honorable mention: "Life is a joke that isn't even funny." "Life is a life sentence that we get for the crime of being born." "Life is a disease for which the only cure is death."

Since the Bible speaks to the deepest interests and needs of humanity, it has much to say about life and living. The words *life, live,* and *living* are found hundreds of times in the biblical revelation.

Persons unfamiliar with the Bible would be surprised at the frankness with which the Bible speaks on this subject. There are lofty passages that set forth positive and ideal concepts of life. There also are honest expressions of cynicism similar to those in the above definitions. For example, Job the sufferer said at one point, " 'I loathe my life' " (Job 10:1).[1] At points the writer of Ecclesiastes echoed the same sentiment, although his cynicism was born of boredom, not suffering (2:17). Even Jacob gave Pharaoh this somewhat cynical estimate of his own life, "Few and evil have been the days of my life" (Gen. 47:9).

Although the Bible honestly reports such views, the overall teaching about life leads to a very different estimate of what life is all about.

A Gift of God

The primary meaning of the Hebrew and Greek words translated life, live, and living is the same as the basic meaning of our English words. "Life" is human existence, physical life as opposed to nonexistence or death. This was Jacob's meaning in Genesis 47:9. Genesis 5 lists the names of numerous early persons. The following formula is used throughout: "So-and-so *lived* so many years, and he died."

Thus the Bible echoes the normal usage of the word "life." However, the Bible views human life from a distinctive point of view: life is seen as the gift of God.

Genesis 1–2 shows God as the Creator who is the source of all life—plants, animals, human beings. Genesis 2:7 uses the two Hebrew words most important for understanding the Old Testament view of life: "Then the Lord God formed man of dust from the ground, and breathed into his nostrils the breath of life [*chaiyim*]; and man became a living being [*nephesh*]." The picture here is of life as breath from God that communicates the vital principle to man and makes him a living being.

Chaiyim is the Hebrew word that corresponds most closely to the English word "life" (Gen. 47:9). The verb form means "live" (Gen. 5:3). The adjective form means "living" (Gen. 2:7). *Nephesh* is one of several Hebrew words that has the basic meaning of breath. Three forms of this root occur in Genesis 2:7: "God *breathed* into his nostrils the *breath* of life; and man became a living *being*." The word can mean breath or that which breathes. Thus the word *nephesh* "is often the equivalent of 'life,' and often of 'person' or 'self,' according as one emphasizes the aliveness of the creature or the creature who is alive." [2]

The King James Version translates *nephesh* in Genesis 2:7 as "soul." This translation emphasizes the unique quality of the life given to man. However, we need to recognize that the same two words translated "living soul" in Genesis 2:7 are used elsewhere of the other "living creatures" made by God (Gen. 1:20,24; 2:19). "Soul" is a legitimate translation if we keep certain facts in mind: "In Hebrew thought man does not have a soul; he *is* a soul. . . . The animals are also souls—in this sense. The difference between man and animals is not in that one is a soul and the others are not, but in the kind of soul that man is. And that is a radical difference!" [3]

Genesis presents human life as distinctive, not by using different words but by describing man's unique relationship to God and to the rest of creation. For example, only man is said to have been created in the image of God (Gen. 1:26-27). Only he has access to the tree of life (2:9). And God appointed man as a trustee with responsibility for the rest of creation (Gen. 1:28). Thus the basic teachings of Genesis 1—2 about life are these: (1) All life—human and nonhuman—is a gift from God; (2) Man has a unique potential for life in fellowship with and obedience to God.

A striking New Testament affirmation of this teaching is found in Paul's speech to the Athenian philosophers. Paul said that God "gives to all men life [zōē] and breath and everything" (Acts 17:25). The word zōē is one of several Greek words for "life" used in the New Testament; in fact it is the word used most frequently. Paul used the verb form of the same word in Acts 17:28 when he affirmed an important result of the fact that life is God's gift to man: "In him [that is God] we live and move and have our being."

The missionary and humanitarian Albert Schweitzer practiced what he called "reverence for life." Beginning with the biblical concept of life as a gift from God, he cultivated a reverence for all life. In these modern and supposedly enlightened times, surely this could be a rallying point for all people of goodwill—a reverence and respect for life.

There are some encouraging signs of a new sensitivity about the value of life, but there also are disheartening facts to show that many people have no reverence for life. The twentieth century dawned amid great hopes of an era of peace and well-being. Tragically the devastation, brutality, and inhumanity practiced by some in this century have been almost unparalleled in history.

Reverence for life implies more than refraining from taking another's most precious possession—his life; it also means a concern for the quality of life. Living life as God's gift means living to the full extent of what it means to be human, a person made in the image of God. Freedom, personhood, and human dignity—all of these are based on life as the gift of God.

Many forces in modern society are working to depersonalize and to dehumanize us. People of faith resist these pressures because they know that human beings are made by God in his image. God made us as persons capable of living with faith, hope, and love.

Viktor Frankl is one of the survivors of Nazi concentration camps. In his book *Man's Search for Meaning,* he tells how the concentration camps were designed to reduce human beings to something less than human. Each prisoner was stripped of all his personal possessions. Even his name was forgotten; he became a number.

These helpless beings were driven about like animals, worked until their strength was gone, then herded into gas chambers and exterminated. The pressure was strong to give in and to become only a thing, a number, an animal. However, some prisoners managed to live and to die as men and women made in God's image.

Frankl notes how the concentration camps thus mirrored the paradox of man in the twentieth century: "After all, man is that being who has invented the gas chambers of Auschwitz; however he is also that being who has entered those gas chambers upright, with the Lord's Prayer or the *Shema Yisrael* on his lips." [4]

More Than Living

Thus we have seen that man's earthly life is a gift from God; we also have seen that this gift imparts a unique potential to human life. The word "life" is used in the Bible many times to refer to man's earthly existence, but the Bible views man's life as much more than the process of living.

Man was made by God and for God. He was made for faith in, fellowship with, and obedience to God. The Old Testament often refers to God as the "living God." One of the meanings of this title is that God is the source of life and that this life is shared with those who know and serve God.

The writer of Psalm 42 (vv. 1-2,8) gave beautiful expression
to his experience with the living God:

> As a hart longs
>   for flowing streams,
> so longs my soul
>   for thee, O God.
> My soul thirsts for God,
>   for the living God.
>
> . . . .
>
> By day the Lord commands his steadfast love;
>   and at night his song is with me,
>   a prayer to the God of my life.

Unfortunately many people know nothing of what the psalmist
meant. They seek life in something other than in a right relationship with the God who made them. Throughout human
history, many people have tried to find ultimate meaning in
earthly existence apart from an acknowledgement or awareness
of God.

This is no merely modern phenomenon. Deuteronomy 8:3
is an ancient warning against this tragic misunderstanding of
life: "Man does not live by bread alone, but . . . by everything
that proceeds out of the mouth of the Lord." As the people
of Israel prepared to enter the Promised Land, they were warned
against becoming so wrapped up in their possessions that they
forgot the Lord (see vv. 11-18).

Jesus quoted Deuteronomy 8:3 when he was locked in spiritual
combat during the wilderness temptations (Matt. 4:4). He quoted
this verse in resisting the temptation to reduce life to the physical
process of living. Jesus could have turned the stones into bread.
He could have satisfied his hunger. He also could have fed many
hungry people using his miraculous power. But Jesus knew that
as basic as is our need for daily bread, our need for the Giver
of the daily bread is even more basic.

Jesus made this same point in teaching his followers how to

live. For instance, in a passage warning against anxiety and preoccupation with things, Jesus asked, "Is not life more than food, and the body more than clothing?" (Matt. 6:25).

His most striking statement on this subject is found in Luke 12:15. A man out of the crowd had asked Jesus, "Teacher, bid my brother divide the inheritance with me" (Luke 12:13). Jesus refused to play the role of judge in this family dispute. Turning to the crowd he said: "Take heed, and beware of all covetousness; for a man's life does not consist in the abundance of his possessions" (Luke 12:15).

Following this statement Jesus told the parable of the rich fool (vv. 16-21). The man in the parable was a hard worker; he surely was not called a fool for this reason. Nor is there any hint that he was dishonest. No, the reason this man was called a fool was because he was so preoccupied with making a living that he missed life as it was intended to be lived. His possessions had become his life; they crowded everything else out. His death revealed the utter folly of his life.

A man's life does not consist in the abundance of his possessions. Nowhere will we find words more relevant than these. For many people, life is little more than the so-called "good things of life" that money will buy.

In the early days of television there was a program called "The Millionaire." In each episode a fabulously wealthy man gave away one million dollars to some unsuspecting person. Few viewers of the show could fail to daydream about what they would do if some unknown benefactor suddenly gave them one million dollars. Most people probably assumed that that much money would solve all their problems. Many episodes of "The Millionaire," as fanciful as the total idea was, were realistic enough to show that wealth can be a mixed blessing. The new wealth solved many problems, but it also created other problems.

There are many things that money will buy, but there also are many things that money cannot buy. Tragically, those who become preoccupied with the former category of needs often ignore the latter category.

Oscar Wilde remarked about a certain man that *he knew the price of everything but the value of nothing.* Such a person is wise in the ways of the world, but he is a fool when it comes to what really counts. He knows the price of everything that can be measured in dollars and cents. But he has little awareness of the real value of those things that are priceless—the very things that this book is about: life, love, hope, joy, peace. Consequently, although he knows how to buy and sell and make a profit, he does not know how to walk with God, to put persons before things, and to enjoy the best that life has to offer.

Man's attempt to find life apart from God has contributed to the deep sense of meaninglessness that pervades so much of modern life and thought. Viktor Frankl has based his approach to psychotherapy on man's search for meaning. Freud emphasized the will to pleasure. Adler spoke of the will to power. Frankl believes that man's will to meaning is more basic. Frankl quotes with approval this statement of Nietzsche: "He who has a *why* to live for can bear almost any *how.*" [5]

When a person has a valid meaning for his life, he can endure much. However, a person who sees little or no meaning to his life is not really living, just existing. This is very close to the theme of the book of Ecclesiastes. The writer tried to find life in a variety of ways. He tried pleasure, possessions, and wisdom. But he did not find the good life he sought. To the contrary he wrote: "So I hated life, because what is done under the sun was grievous to me; for all is vanity and a striving after wind" (Eccl. 2:17).

Ian Fleming was the writer of the James Bond stories. Shortly before his death, someone asked Fleming what it was like to be famous. The author replied: "Well . . . I suppose it was all right for a bit—nice being known in restaurants and having people take notice of you. But now, my God! Ashes, old boy—just ashes!"

Suppose that a person from a remote area of the world saw a piano for the first time. He might ask, "What's that?" Someone could say, "That's a piano." Then the visitor might ask, "What's it for?" He might assume by looking that a piano is primarily a decorative piece of furniture. It is that, but it is much more. Suppose someone answered the visitor's question by playing some music on the piano. Then the visitor would know what the piano is for.

We look at a human being. The psalmist asked, "What is man?" (Ps. 8:4.). Someone could answer by giving the proper anthropological name for the human species. And he could go on to describe human life from a physical and biological point of view. And man is all of this—just as the piano is a decorative piece of furniture. But just as a piano is more than a piece of furniture, so is man more than *homo sapiens.* The crucial question is not "What is man's name?" or "How is he put together?" but "What is he for?" The proper place to begin answering this question is the Bible. According to the Bible, man's purpose is bound up with the intention of his Creator.

A Matter of Life and Death

The heart of the human problem, at least as far as the Bible is concerned, is that man has a persistent determination to try to find life on his own terms, not in relationship with God. In biblical terminology this is the basic sin of mankind.

Jeremiah 2:12-13 provides a graphic picture of the folly of man's turning from God:

> Be appalled, O heavens, at this,
> be shocked, be utterly desolate, says the Lord,
> for my people have committed two evils:
> they have forsaken me,
> the fountain of living waters,
> and hewed out cisterns for themselves,

broken cisterns,
    that can hold no water.

God is here vividly portrayed as the source of life. He is compared to a fresh, life-giving spring. Yet the people of Judah had turned from God to idols. This was like forsaking a never-failing spring for man-made cisterns. A cistern is at best inferior to a spring; but to make matters worse, these cisterns leak. Therefore, when the thirsty people come to their cisterns, they will find no water.

Modern man has made idols of many things. He assumes that he has outgrown any need of God. He trusts himself, his resources, and devices. But the things in which he has placed his trust can neither slake his thirst nor give him life. Only God can do that.

The Bible views this as a life-or-death issue. The consequences of turning from God are often described in terms of death as opposed to life. For example, Deuteronomy 30 describes this as the choice God set before the Israelites as they prepared to enter the Promised Land (vv. 15,19-20). If they trusted and obeyed God, they would live. If they turned from God, they would die.

The Old Testament views physical death as a consequence of man's sin. The ancient Hebrews viewed long life as evidence of faith and obedience. However, the contrast between life and death increasingly came to be understood as meaning more than a contrast between a long life and a short life. The quality of life with God came to be emphasized, and death came to be seen as separation from God. By New Testament times the concepts of eternal life and the second death had been revealed to people of faith.

Even before the full revelation of life in Christ, the offer of life was extended to those who had turned their backs on God. The Old Testament viewed man as a sinner under the condemnation of death. However, God offered life to those who were already living in the ways of death.

This good news prior to the Christian good news was especially prominent in the messages of the prophets. Amos, whose message was primarily one of judgment, called on the sinful people of Israel to "seek the Lord and live" (5:6; see also 5:4,14). Ezekiel was even more emphatic in issuing this urgent invitation from God: "As I live, says the Lord God, I have no pleasure in the death of the wicked, but that the wicked turn from his way and live; turn back, turn back from your evil ways; for why will you die, O house of Israel?" (33:11; see the entire passage, vv. 1-16). Isaiah 55:1-3 comes even closer to the New Testament gospel of salvation by grace:

> Ho, every one who thirsts,
>   come to the waters;
> and he who has no money,
>   come, buy and eat!
> Come, buy wine and milk
>   without money and without price.
> Why do you spend your money for that which is not bread,
>   and your labor for that which does not satisfy?
> Hearken diligently to me, and eat what is good,
>   and delight yourselves in fatness.
> Incline your ear, and come to me;
>   hear, that your soul may live.

The New Testament makes this good news explicit and clear. Life apart from God is spiritual death; God in Christ came to raise us from spiritual death to spiritual life (Eph. 2:1). The person who repents and believes passes from death to life (John 5:24). One of the best summaries of the life-and-death issues involved in responding to the gospel is found in Romans 6:23: "For the wages of sin is death, but the free gift of God is eternal life through Christ Jesus our Lord."

This message of life is good news to those who know they need God's mercy and grace. Many people turn a deaf ear to

God's invitation, because they do not think of themselves as persons who need God's grace. Some of them are willing to concede that the Christian gospel may be good news for people who are out-and-out sinners. But they see themselves as decent, respectable people who do not fit into that category.

Suppose you and I hear on the radio that a ship is sinking far out at sea. Rescue planes and ships are reported to be on the way. Then several hours later we hear the news that all hands have been rescued. That would be good news, and we would be glad to hear it.

But suppose for a moment that we are among those needing to be rescued. We are in danger of losing life itself. Then someone shouts, "Look, a plane. We're saved!" The words "good news" could not begin to describe how *good* that news would be to us, because that news would spell the difference between life and death for us personally—not someone else's life or death but yours and mine!

The good news of God's offer of life to sinners should sound just as good. No one who is honest with himself can stand aside and listen to the good news as if it were not for him personally. This is a matter of life and death—for each of us.

Finding Life in Christ

The Gospel of John is the most important Christian writing on the meaning of "life." The word *zōē* is found thirty-six times in John and only sixteen times in the other three Gospels. In John the word *zōē* never refers to our natural life that ends at death. When John wanted to refer to the physical life, he used another word *psychē* (13:37; 15:13). *Zōē,* however, was used by the Greeks and also at times in other New Testament books to refer to physical life. John thus used the normal word for man's most precious possession to point to that new, abundant, and eternal life that God offers us in Christ.

John stated his purpose for writing in terms of "life": "that you may believe that Jesus is the Christ, the Son of God, and that believing you may have life in his name" (20:31). Throughout the Gospel the word "life" is bound up with what God offers men in Christ. At the beginning, John states of Christ the Word that "in him was life" (1:4). "As the Father has life in himself, so he has granted the Son also to have life in himself" (5:26).

Among the characteristics of John's Gospel are the "I am" statements of Jesus. Nowhere are the unique claims for Jesus Christ set forth more clearly than in John's Gospel. And these titles for Christ are often stated using the word "life." Jesus said: "I am the bread of life" (6:35); "I am the resurrection and the life" (11:25); "I am the way, and the truth, and the life" (14:6).

Many people today are offended by such statements as these. They want to accept Jesus on their terms, not his. They deny that Jesus was the Son of God; instead they claim that he was a good man—probably the best, and a great teacher—very likely the greatest.

Men like Elton Trueblood, C. S. Lewis, and J. B. Phillips have pointed to a basic flaw in this position: This position overlooks the radical claims of Christ about who he is and what he came to do. Either Christ spoke the truth, or he did not. If he spoke the truth, he is much more than a good man and a great teacher. If he did not speak the truth, he was neither a good man nor a great teacher. Good men and great teachers do not build their lives and teachings on a lie.

Some people deny that Jesus ever really made such claims as those found in John's Gospel. They insist that the early church is responsible for transforming a good man who taught about God into the divine Son of God. They believe that Jesus was only an earnest man trying to teach God's love. Then the church transformed him in its thinking into the Son of God and Savior of the world.

Elton Trueblood is one of many Christian scholars who insists that we can trust the New Testament witness to Christ. The Bible does accurately represent the mind of Christ, not merely the opinion of early believers. In his book *A Place to Stand,* Trueblood writes: "There is no good reason why the ordinary Christian should be intimidated by the confident assertions of men who claim to know definitely which parts of the Gospel record are original and which were added as a result of the needs and experience of the early Church." [6]

Trueblood believes that the New Testament doctrine of Christ is confirmed by the Christian experience with Christ. The evidence of changed lives is difficult to refute. "The evidence of lives changed by contact with Christ is so abundant that the full story can never be told; it is, indeed, of a kind not matched anywhere in any culture. The changed lives have come about, not primarily by a set of ideas or by acceptance of a doctrine, but by commitment to a Person." [7]

Therefore, no Christian needs to be hesitant about accepting such radical claims as the "I am" statements attributed to Jesus in John's Gospel. He is the unique life-bearer and life-giver. Because he is the source of life, he is able to give this life to those who commit themselves to him and to his way.

One of the most striking incidents recorded in John is found in John 4:1-42. Jesus' encounter with the woman at the well illustrates how Christ imparts life to others. The woman had been married five times. When Jesus met her, she was living with a man who was not her husband. She had no doubt become disillusioned with life after so many failures. Yet, Jesus believed that life could begin again for this woman; he spoke to her about "living water" (v. 10).

Since the conversation had begun with Jesus asking her for a drink of water, she assumed at first that Jesus was speaking of physical water. Then Jesus explained by contrasting the living water with the water from the well: "Every one who drinks of this water will thirst again, but whoever drinks of the water that I shall give him will never thirst; the water that I shall give him will become in him a well of water welling up to eternal life" (vv. 13-14).

As they continued to talk, Jesus used the "I am" formula to claim that he was the Messiah. The woman left her water pot and hurried into the village to tell what had happened. Others came, heard Jesus, and believed in him as the Savior of the world.

Christians often use the slogan "Christ is the answer." What do they mean by this? Jesus' dealings with the woman at the well can help show in what way Jesus is the answer.

Let us first note what we do *not* mean by "Christ is the answer." We do not mean that Christ changes the past. Nothing could change the fact of what the woman's past had been. Even after meeting Christ she would have to continue to live with some of the inevitable consequences of the past. Neither do we mean that Christ is the answer in the sense of assuring easy solutions for future problems. Christ does not promise an easy future to new converts; to the contrary he warns Christians to expect their share of troubles.

In what sense then is Christ the answer? Another way to ask the question is this: In what sense does Christ give a person *new* life? First of all, Christ forgives the guilt of our sins. He does not change the past, but he does set us free from the chains of past sins. He breaks the power that the past has to haunt us and to humiliate us. And Christ also brings us into a new relationship with God. The presence of his Spirit with us is the life-giving water that refreshes and revitalizes. Because of his presence with us, the future is bound to be different.

Jesus used a different analogy to teach the same truth when he spoke to Nicodemus about the new birth (John 3:1-8). The new life Christ gives to a person is not just another chance; it is a *new* life. Those who believe in reincarnation teach another chance through the rebirth of the soul into another lifetime. However, this would not solve our basic problem: We would still essentially be living our lives on the same human level. John and Paul refer to this as life in the *flesh*. This means a life lived apart from God from purely human resources and impulses. What Jesus gives believers is a new kind of life, a life in fellowship with God. The Spirit of God is the vitalizing force of this life. This new birth is not just a new start; it is a new life.

Living by Dying

Three adjectives help describe the life that Christ gives: *new, abundant,* and *eternal.* The second of these is based on John 10:10 where Jesus said, "I came that they may have life, and have it abundantly." The word "abundantly" has the meaning of fullness. Christ gives to us a rich, full life in the best sense of the words.

When she was a baby, Helen Keller was rendered blind and deaf by near-fatal illness. When she was almost seven years old, a new person entered her life—a person destined to change her life. Anne Sullivan had come to teach Helen—to open the lines of communication into and out of Helen's dark, silent existence. Miss Sullivan tried to help Helen learn that each object has a name. She did this by making the letters of a word in the child's hand. At first Helen thought that this was only a new game. Eventually she was able to perceive that certain marks made on her hand meant certain objects, but she continued to be confused about most objects. For example, she persisted in confusing the words "mug" and "water."

One day Anne Sullivan took Helen to the well house. Someone was drawing water. The teacher thrust the child's hand under the cool liquid gushing forth. At the same time she wrote the word "water" in Helen's other hand, first slowly, then rapidly. Helen Keller tells what happened then:

I stood still, my whole attention fixed upon the movements of her fingers. Suddenly I felt a misty consciousness as of something forgotten—a thrill of returning thought; and somehow the mystery of language returned to me. I knew then that "w-a-t-e-r" meant the wonderful cool something that flowed over my hand. That living word awakened my soul, gave it light, hope, joy, set it free! [8]

Helen Keller's experience is a true parable of what Jesus Christ does for us. Christ offers us the key that unlocks the way to a full and meaningful life.

Christ is the center around which Christians live their lives. Paul wrote, "For to me to live is Christ" (Phil. 1:21). Paul lived his life out of a personal relationship with God through Christ. Christ had provided for Paul the key to what makes life worth living. Jesus' example and teachings point the way; his abiding Spirit gives the motivation and power.

An excellent summary of Paul's view of life is found in Galatians 2:20: "I have been crucified with Christ; it is no longer I who live, but Christ who lives in me; and the life I now live in the flesh I live by faith in the Son of God, who loved me and gave himself for me."

This view of life is shot through with paradox. Part of the paradox is the tension between the freedom of self-expression and the surrender of all to Christ. Paul's view might at first seem to lead to a complete loss of personal identity and freedom of expression. However, the exact opposite is true. Paul was never more completely himself, in the best sense of the term, than when his life was centered in Christ.

Christ provides the key for living life as it was intended to be lived. Every person's life revolves around some center. God is the center around which life was intended to revolve. If he made us for himself, this is only reasonable. God in Christ provides that new orientation that puts all things in proper perspective. Life in Christ thus is abundant, full life.

Another part of the paradox is the concept of living by dying. Paul spoke of being crucified with Christ, yet living. Jesus stated this principle in its most paradoxical form: "Whoever would save his life will lose it, and whoever loses his life for my sake will find it" (Matt. 16:24). Jesus made this statement in connection with his challenge for men to deny themselves, take up their crosses, and follow him. The dying about which he spoke thus had to do with a willingness to lay down one's life for the sake of God and others. Crossbearing and self-denial speak to the need not only to lay down our lives in *dying* but also to lay down our lives in *living*.

The tendency of us all is to center our lives around ourselves, to let our own narrow circle of selfish interests and concerns control our actions. Many people know no other way to live. Jesus never depreciated the importance of self-esteem and personal individuality, but he taught that "self" should be in proper relation to God and others. When a person makes his decisions only in the light of self-interest and self-preservation, he misses the very life he is so intent on finding and clinging to. Only as a person learns to give of himself for God and others does he truly begin to live. Thus in a sense, he lives by dying.

> "A man must live!" We justify
> Low shift and trick, to treason high;
> A little vote for a little gold,
> Or a whole Senate bought and sold,
> With this self-evident reply—
>   "A man must live!"
>
> But is it so? Pray tell me why
> Life at such cost you have to buy.
> In what religion were you told
> A man must live?
> There are times when a man must die!
> There are times when a man will die!
> Imagine for a battle-cry
> From soldiers with a sword to hold,

> From soldiers with a flag unfurled,
> This coward's whine, this liar's lie,
>   "A man must live!"
>
> The Savior did not "live!"
> He died!
> But in his death was life—
> And we, being crucified
> Afresh with him, may find
> Life in the cup of death,
> And, drinking it,
>   Win life forever more.[9]

The death and resurrection of Jesus are more than doctrines to be believed; they are the pattern and power of abundant Christian living. The Spirit of the crucified and risen Lord within a believer enables him to die to a selfish way of living and empowers him to live for God and others.

Earlier in the chapter, reference was made to modern man's search for meaning. Evidences abound that life for many people is empty and meaningless. Many people are literally dying for lack of something to live for. In their frantic scramble for life, many people have missed it completely. Among those whose lives are emptiest are those who have all that most of us assume would guarantee a rich, full life—wealth, success, good times.

By contrast, others take seriously the way of Christian discipleship set forth by Jesus. By losing life, they have found it. By giving themselves away, they have discovered themselves for the first time. By dying, they are living. Life for such people is often difficult, sometimes discouraging, at times dangerous; but life is never empty and dull. Christ gives life its true meaning.

Life That Overcomes Death

John Redhead tells of a small boy who wrote a letter to an American chaplain serving in France during World War I. The boy, who was just learning to express himself in writing, closed with these words: "I send you my love, and I hope you will live all your life." [10] That is precisely what the abundant life in Christ is all about—living all your life. However, Christ also promises that this new, abundant life will never end. Death will not extinguish life in Christ; to the contrary death will only enlarge its possibilities.

Much has been written and said about the modern tendency to deny death. Society has gone to great lengths to avoid the reality of death. Someone has observed that whereas the word "sex" was taboo a few generations ago, now the word "death" is taboo.

This situation seems to be improving. More and more voices have been raised protesting society's denial of death. More and more people are aware that denying our mortality is unhealthy and self-defeating. In reaching this conclusion people are moving closer to the biblical position about life and death.

The writers of the Bible were very aware of death. The shortness of life and the certainty of death are frequent biblical themes. The letter of James, for example, warns against presuming on always having a tomorrow in which to complete the plans of today. James wrote: "What is your life? For you are a mist that appears for a little time and then vanishes" (Jas. 4:14).

Mortality was particularly threatening in Old Testament times. The ancient Hebrews had little or no concept of life beyond death. Only toward the end of the Old Testament period were people beginning to express a hope of life after death. The words "everlasting life" are found only once in the Old Testament—in Daniel 12:2.

By contrast, life after death is a recurring theme in the New Testament. Genesis tells how sin blocked man's way to the tree of life. The book of Revelation pictures paradise restored. The new heaven and the new earth will be inhabited by those whose names "are written in the Lamb's book of life" (21:27). They have access to the "tree of life" (22:2). Believers are to invite all who will to "take the water of life without price" (22:17).

This promise of life is based not on wishful thinking but on Christ's victory over death. Near the beginning of Revelation, the Lord of glory says to John: "Fear not, I am the first and the last, and the living one; I died, and behold I am alive for evermore, and I have the keys of Death and Hades" (1:17-18).

The word "life" in the New Testament is frequently used together with the word "eternal." This is particularly true in John's Gospel. The qualifying adjective *aiōnios* used with *zōē* means literally pertaining to an *aiōn* or age. The Hebrews had thought of the Messiah's coming as introducing a new age—the age to come. Thus eternal life (*aiōnios zōē*) referred to the life of the age to come. This life is a reality for those who know Christ, and it will continue to be a reality even beyond death.

Thus, "eternal life" represents both the quality and the quantity of life in Christ. It is *everlasting* life, but it is first of all *life*. John repeatedly emphasizes the present reality of eternal life. One definition of eternal life is stated in John 17:3; Jesus' prayer included these words: "This is eternal life, that they know thee the only true God, and Jesus Christ whom thou hast sent."

John Baillie in his book *And the Life Everlasting* tells of J.M.E. McTaggart, an atheist who set out to prove the immortality of the soul. McTaggart insisted that he had no room in his life or thought for God, but he was strongly attracted by the idea of heaven. So he went to great lengths to prove heaven and to disprove God. Baillie correctly observes: "To speak of *heaven* without *God* is to depart entirely from the accepted meaning of the term. What McTaggart did, if he did anything, was to prove the existence of hell and the nonexistence of heaven." [11]

Baillie's point is well taken: everlasting existence without God is not what the Bible calls heaven, but hell. The presence of God is the difference between life and death and between heaven and hell. What makes eternal life so inviting, first of all, is not that it is *everlasting* but that it is *life*.

But the double blessing of eternal life is that it is both—it is life and it is everlasting. When Jesus was explaining why he was the Bread of life, he said: "I am the living bread which came down from heaven; if anyone eats of this bread, he will live for ever" (John 6:51). When Jesus spoke to Martha after the death of Lazarus, he said: "I am the resurrection and the life; he who believes in me, though he die, yet shall he live, and whoever lives and believes in me shall never die' " (John 11:25-26). Jesus promises, "Because I live, you will live also" (John 14:19).

This assurance of victory over death was a strong influence on the attitudes and actions of the early Christian believers. They did not need to *deny* death; through Christ they actually could *defy* death. Being set free from the fear of death enabled them to live life with courage. Earthly life was no less precious to them than to others, but they were willing to risk their very lives for Christ's sake. Death for them was not the last act of life; it was only the door to continued life with God. Thus death was not the ultimate tragedy; failing Christ was the ultimate tragedy.

Paul is a good example of this point of view. His words in Philippians 1:19-26 are an excellent statement of a Christian philosophy of life and death. At the center of Paul's testimony are the words: "For to me to live is Christ, and to die is gain" (v. 21). The other verses show what he meant: Paul's life was centered in Christ. His goal was to honor Christ in all things and at all times. Thus he prayed that he would honor Christ both by how he lived and by how he died. Paul was ready to live for Christ, and he was ready to die for Christ. He was willing to leave the time and circumstances of his death in God's hand. Death held no fears for him; in fact, departing to be with the Lord was an inviting prospect. However, Paul was not morbid nor was he so otherworldly that he had no concern for his earthly life. To the contrary, he lived life to the full as he sought to serve God and others. This is a healthy, Christian attitude toward life and toward death. (See chapter 3 for more on the hope of eternal life.)

Summary

1. Physical life is a gift of God. All life is precious, human life especially so because man has a unique potential for life in fellowship with God.

2. Since man was made by God and for God, he finds life's true purpose in doing God's will. Life thus is much more than the process of living.

3. Man's persistent problem is turning from God and life. This is what the Bible calls sin, and the wages of sin is death. In spite of man's sin, God in mercy calls men to find life in him.

4. Christ as the Son of God is the bearer of life and the giver of new life. He breaks the power of the past over a person and sets the person free to live a new life with God.

5. Christ offers a full, abundant life. The secret of this life is in the paradox of living by dying—living for God and others by dying to a life dominated by selfishness.

6. Life in Christ is not only new and abundant; it also is eternal. Christ has conquered death. He imparts this same victory to those who share with him in the way of the cross.

---

[1] Unless otherwise indicated, the Bible quotations are from the Revised Standard Version.

[2] Derek Kidner, *Genesis* (Chicago: Inter-varsity Press, 1967), p. 61.

[3] Clyde Francisco, *The Broadman Bible Commentary,* Vol. 1 revised (Nashville: Broadman Press, 1973), p. 125.

[4] Viktor E. Frankl, *Man's Search for Meaning* (New York: Washington Square Press, 1963), pp. 213-14.

[5] *Ibid.,* p. 164.

[6] Elton Trueblood, *A Place to Stand* (New York: Harper & Row, 1969), p. 51.

[7] *Ibid.,* p. 43.

[8] Helen Keller, *The Story of My Life* (New York: Doubleday and Co., Inc.,

1947), p. 23.

[9] Charlotte Stetson Gilman, "A Man Must Live," *Masterpieces of Religious Verse,* ed. James Dalton Morrison (New York: Harper & Row, 1948), p. 225.

[10] John A. Redhead, *Living All Your Life* (Nashville: Abingdon Press, 1961), p. 7.

[11] (New York: Charles Scribner's Sons, 1933), p. 113.

love —what the world needs now 2

Imagine that you are a newcomer to America and that you are in the process of learning the English language. In how many different ways might you hear and see the word "love" being used?

A child eating an ice-cream cone smacks his lips and says, "I just love ice cream." The sign outside a movie theater advertises a "loverama" double feature, which is filled with sex and passion. A newspaper story on Brotherhood Week quotes a spokesman as urging everyone to love his fellowman. On television a preacher speaks on the Bible text "God is love." A newcomer surely would be confused as he tried to decide what the word "love" means.

Although there is little agreement about the exact meaning of "love," nearly everyone agrees that love is what the world needs now. The ambiguity of the word creates some confusion, but the general agreement on the priority of love does at least provide a point of contact for diverse points of view.

"Four-letter words" are increasingly a part of modern life and speech. When we speak of "four-letter words," we usually mean profane, vulgar words. However, "love" is surely the most popular four-letter word—not only among Christians but also among those who use many of the other kind of four-letter words.

The Bible is an indispensable guide in discovering what love is all about. Christianity is essentially a religion of love—not just an otherworldly love but a love that gets down to where people really live. Christians, therefore, need to make the most of this point of contact with modern society. We need to be aggressive in presenting and in practicing what the Bible teaches about love.

Friend or Foe?

G. A. Studdert-Kennedy, the English chaplain-poet, told how he stood one night on the cliffs of Dover, peering out into the darkness across the English Channel. He was pondering what kind of force moved there in the darkness. What really lies behind the universe? Is the universe indifferent to human life and needs, or is there an unseen Force that has purpose and concern? Is there really a God, and does he care for us? As he pondered these questions, he recalled the experiences of sentries on night duty during World War I. A sentry peers anxiously into the darkness when he hears someone approaching. The sentry asks, "Who goes there, friend or foe?" What a relief when he hears the answer "friend." At Dover on that dark night Studdert-Kennedy asked the same question of the unseen Force moving in the darkness, "Who goes there, friend or foe?" He dared to believe that the answer was "Friend."

From a biblical point of view, the ability of a person to love and trust is based on his trust in a God who loves and cares. The person who dares to believe that "God is love" (1 John 4:8,16) is best equipped to express love to others.

Believing in a God of love takes faith, but it is not "blind" faith. Trust in God is in response to events that the Bible interprets as revelations of God's love. There are many people who refuse to believe in a loving God; they point to things that seem to them to deny the existence of such a God. The writers of the Bible were not unaware of the unexplained suffering, evil, and injustices of life. Therefore, they did not glibly conclude that "God is love." They came to this belief on the basis of what they believed to be the hand of a loving God in human history and experience.

The Old Testament interprets God's covenant with Israel as evidence of his love. Hosea 11:1-4 gives God's word about his love for Israel:

> When Israel was a child, I loved him,
>   and out of Egypt I called my son.
> The more I called them,
>   the more they went from me;
> they kept sacrificing to the Baals,
>   and burning incense to idols.
> Yet it was I who taught Ephraim to walk,
>   I took them up in my arms;
>   but they did not know that I healed them.
> I led them with cords of compassion,
>   with the bands of love.

The usual Hebrew word for love was *ahabah.* Like our English word "love," *ahabah* could refer to divine love or to human love. When used of God's love, the word refers to a love based on God's nature as love, not on the lovable nature of those whom he loves.

Deuteronomy 7:7-8 probes the question, "Why did the Lord choose Israel?" The writer specifically denied that the reason lay in some characteristic of Israel that explains God's choice. He explained God's choice solely in terms of God's love for Israel: "It was not because you were more in number than any other people that the Lord set his love upon you and chose you, for you were the fewest of all peoples; but it is because the Lord loves you." In other words, God chose them because he loved them. Why did he love them? He loved them because that is the kind of God he is.

Norman H. Snaith in *The Distinctive Ideas of the Old Testament* refers to *ahabah* as God's election love. He distinguishes this kind of love from another Hebrew word *chesed,* which refers to God's covenant love. *Ahabah* is God's unconditioned love that explains his election or choice of Israel. Without this love there would be no covenant. *Chesed* is God's loyal love in entering into and maintaining his covenant with Israel. *Chesed* is usually translated as "lovingkindness" in the King James Version and as "steadfast love" in the Revised Standard Version.

Chesed is found twice in Exodus 34:6-7, one of the most important Old Testament revelations of God. This revelation came after the Israelites had entered into and broken the covenant at Sinai. Moses asked God to renew the covenant. In the process God proclaimed this as his name: "The Lord, the Lord, a God merciful and gracious, slow to anger, and abounding in steadfast love and faithfulness, keeping steadfast love for thousands, forgiving iniquity and transgression and sin, but who will by no means clear the guilty, visiting the iniquity of the fathers upon the children and the children's children, to the third and fourth generation."

Throughout Israel's history the prophets continued to wrestle with the problem of whether God could remain true to Israel even though Israel proved untrue to God. The themes of judgment and mercy are intertwined in the prophetic writings. The theme of God's love shines through most clearly in Hosea. God led Hosea to see a parallel between his own relationship to his unfaithful wife Gomer and God's relationship to unfaithful Israel. Out of the crucible of his own anguish, frustration, and love, Hosea came to new insight about God's love for disobedient Israel. God commanded Hosea to love Gomer "even as the Lord loves the people of Israel" (Hos. 3:1). Because God's love for Israel was based on God's nature, not Israel's goodness, God continued to love his people, even in spite of their sins.

In Marc Connelly's play *Green Pastures* he dramatizes a black child's conception of Old Testament history. As the story of the people's persistent sin unfolds, God leaves them to their own devices and vows not to come again to their aid. But as time passes, God in heaven cannot be content to ignore the cries of his people. A man named Hosea keeps walking past his office door; and each time Hosea passes, God hears a far-off cry for help. So God decides to go to earth once again to see what is happening. He talks with a man who tells him of God's love. When God (who is pretending to be an old country preacher) asks the man how he knows that God is love, the man tells him that Hosea told them so. Further conversation reveals that Hosea learned this through suffering.

Although the child's conception of Old Testament history is a little garbled, it contains many true insights: God did not learn of love from Hosea; Hosea simply saw more clearly what has always been true of God. However, the connection between love and suffering is certainly true. *Green Pastures* closes with God pondering the thought of God himself suffering. The final scene foreshadows the crucifixion of Jesus—where the suffering love of God is revealed most clearly.

What was dimly perceived by some under the old covenant burst into full glory in the coming, life, death, and resurrection of Jesus Christ: "For God so loved the world that he gave his only Son, that whoever believes in him should not perish but have eternal life" (John 3:16). "In this is love, not that we loved God but that he loved us and sent his Son to be the expiation for our sins" (1 John 4:10).

The Greek word *agapē* is used to describe this self-giving love of God. As in the choice of Israel, the reason for the coming of Christ is not to be found in man's nature but in God's. Jesus did not come because humanity deserved divine help; Jesus was sent because God is love. His very nature is to love.

John, who gives special emphasis to God's love, highlights the love of God the Father and God the Son as the basis for God's love for mankind. Jesus, in his high priestly prayer, voiced this prayer: "That the world may know that thou hast sent me and hast loved them even as thou hast loved me" (John 17:23). Jesus spoke to the Father of what he called "thy love for me before the foundation of the world" (John 17:24). This is another way of saying that God's love for humanity is but a reflection of him whose very nature is love. God is eternally love, prior to and apart from his love for us.

Romans 5:5-8 clearly states the way God's love comes to us. Verse 5 tells how "God's love has been poured into our hearts through the Holy Spirit which has been given to us." Verses 6-8 tell of the revelation of God's love in Christ's death: "While we were yet helpless, at the right time Christ died for the ungodly. Why, one will hardly die for a righteous man—though perhaps for a good man one will dare even to die. But God shows his love for us in that while we were yet sinners Christ died for us."

This clearly shows that God's *agapē* was given not because we deserved help but because God loved us. The condition of mankind is described as helpless, ungodly, and sinners. Christ died for us "while we were yet sinners."

Notice also how Paul states this: "*God* shows his love for us in that . . . Christ died for us." The death of Christ is seen as the revelation of God's love. There is no separation of Christ's love and God's love. They are one and the same. When Paul spoke of "the love of Christ," he meant the same thing as "the love of God in Christ Jesus our Lord" (Rom. 8:35,39).

A child said: "I love Jesus, but I don't like God." Someone had not accurately interpreted the Christian view of Jesus to the child. Somehow he had gotten the impression that Jesus is warm, human, and concerned; but God is stern, distant, and unconcerned. The Christian view is that God is exactly what we see reflected in the actions of Jesus Christ—in his teachings, in his acts of compassion, in his suffering and death.

A. Leonard Griffith tells of viewing in the Louvre a dramatic painting by Eugene Carrière:

As you come upon it, it seems to be a mere blending of shadows and darkness. Nothing seems to break the unrelieved night. As you walk closer, you see vaguely the outline of a Cross hidden behind the veil of shadows. Then as you look longer, you become strangely aware that behind the Cross are the dim outlines of a figure with hands outstretched, holding the Cross, and the agony on the face hidden by the shadows is more terrible than the agony of the face of him who hangs on the Cross.[1]

The Test of True Religion

An actor was being interviewed on the radio. He is one of the regulars in a popular television series. The actor was relating the guiding philosophy of the series—an underlying concern for people as people. The main characters in the series are irreligious, but are genuinely concerned for people. They do battle each week with various forces that tend to reduce persons to things.

This series presents a popular philosophy of life—humanism. Humanism is the prevailing mood of our times. Humanism seeks to practice "Christian" morality and compassion without Christian faith. Many humanists are among the most vocal advocates of love for other persons, but humanists deny that God or religion has anything to do with showing love for others. Humanists argue that whether or not a person believes in God is irrelevant to whether or not he shows love for other people. Humanists in fact make the charge that religion has often been a force that hinders rather than motivates concern for persons.

Christians agree with humanists that love for other persons demands top priority, but we believe that experiencing God's love is the most valid source of a continuing concern for other persons. We admit that religion and religious people have sometimes been guilty of lovelessness and callous disregard for persons. However, such religion is not worthy of the name "Christian." In fact, what some people call "religion" the Bible calls *sin*.

The New Testament ties together our love for God and our love for other people. Jesus was asked, "Which is the great commandment of the law?" He replied: "You shall love the

Lord your God with all your heart, with all your soul, and with all your mind. This is the great and first commandment. And a second is like it, You shall love your neighbor as yourself. On these two commandments depend all the law and the prophets" (Matt. 22:36-40; see also Mark 12:28-33). Jesus quoted from two Old Testament passages—Deuteronomy 6:5 and Leviticus 19:18.

The quotation from Deuteronomy is part of the *Shema,* the Hebrew's confession of faith in Deuteronomy 6:4-5. This is one of many Old Testament admonitions to love God. The *Shema* stresses the totality of commitment involved in loving God. The Israelites worshiped one God in contrast to the many gods worshiped by other nations. That one God demanded whole-hearted allegiance.

Jesus quoted the *Shema* as the great commandment of the law, and he added to it the words of Leviticus 19:18. By doing this he linked together love for God and love for others. The commandments of the Old Testament have to do with right attitudes and actions toward God and toward other people. Thus both aspects of love are a part of the Christian response to these relationships.

The early Christians recognized the importance of this saying of Jesus. In two of Paul's most important letters the apostle quoted Leviticus 19:18 as summing up the entire law. In Romans 13:8-10 he wrote:

> Owe no one anything, except to love one another; for he who loves his neighbor has fulfilled the law. The commandments, "You shall not commit adultery, You shall not kill, You shall not steal, You shall not covet," and any other commandment, are summed up in this sentence, "You shall love your neighbor as yourself." Love does no wrong to a neighbor; therefore love is the fulfilling of the law.

Paul made the same point in Galatians 5:14. And James 2:8 refers to Leviticus 19:18 as "the royal law."

John's writings provide an even closer linking of a Christian's love to God and his love to others. John hammered away relentlessly at these two points: (1) Our love for others grows out of our experience of God's love for us; (2) The person who does not love his brother knows nothing of the Father's love. Notice how both these ideas are found in 1 John 4:19-21:

> We love, because he first loved us. If any one says, "I love God," and hates his brother, he is a liar; for he who does not love his brother whom he has seen, cannot love God whom he has not seen. And this commandment we have from him, that he who loves God should love his brother also.

One of the great tragedies of life is the loveless spirit of many professing Christians. Jesus rebuked some of his contemporaries for majoring on minors. They had been careful to tithe the smallest herbs in their gardens, but they had neglected "justice and the love of God" (Luke 11:42). Nothing is such a denial of a professed faith in God than a loveless spirit toward others. Nothing is such a denial of everything Christ stands for. Jesus taught that a person cannot accept Christ and reject humanity (Matt. 25:31-46).

Someone observed a sign that epitomizes the contradiction between what we profess and what we practice. The sign on the property of a religious order read:

KEEP OUT
SISTERS OF MERCY

No wonder the humanists can smugly ignore God when those who believe in God show so little of God's love. Actions more than arguments are much more likely to convince humanists that God is the source of all real concern. Christians have many opportunities to join hands with others in acts of concern toward persons. There are many reasons why we should be quick to join in such efforts.

One reason is the crying need of people for all kinds of help.

Can we afford not to join hands with all men of goodwill in ministries to people? A three-year-old child wandered away from her rural home and became lost. A plea went out for help and many responded. All day they searched the fields and woods for miles around, but to no avail. On the morning of the second day someone suggested joining hands and making a series of concentrated sweeps through the area. They found the child's body in a gully. She had fallen and hit her head on a rock. She was dead. One of the men tenderly picked up the child and carried the limp, little body to the distraught mother. Hysterically the mother cried out: "Why didn't you join hands sooner—why didn't you join hands sooner?" Many urgent human needs will not begin to be met until all people of concern join hands.

When Christians diligently participate in cooperative ventures, and when we faithfully perform our distinctive Christian ministries, the world takes note. And when they take note, they will be forced to take seriously our claims that the God of love is the reason for what love we show others. "We love, because he first loved us" (1 John 4:19).

E. Stanley Jones, the well-known Methodist missionary to India, once said to Gandhi that he would like to see Christianity play a larger role in the national life of India. He asked Gandhi, "What would you suggest that we do to make that possible?" This was Gandhi's candid reply: "I would suggest, first, that all of you Christians must begin to live more like Jesus Christ. Second, I would suggest that you must practice your religion without adulterating or toning it down. Third, I would suggest that you must put your emphasis upon love, for love is the center and soul of Christianity."

Turning Life Inside Out

During the bloody Civil War battle of Shiloh, Abraham Lincoln hastened to the War Department to hear reports from the battlefield. He met the brother and sister-in-law of General Lew Wallace, who was at Shiloh. Seeing Lincoln, the sister-in-law said: "We had heard that a General Wallace was among the killed, and we were afraid it was *our* Wallace. But it wasn't."

"Ah," Lincoln replied, looking down into her face with sad eyes, "but it was *somebody's* Wallace."

Our lives tend to become circumscribed by a tight circle of our own concerns to the exclusion of others. Christian love seeks not only to enlarge that circle but also to turn it inside out until our focus is not on ourselves but on others.

Unlike modern English, the Greek language of the first century had several words to express various facets of love. The word *eros* sometimes was used of sexual love and sometimes of the love for whatever is attractive, desirable, lovable. The word *philia* meant a warm affection for others. Another word for love, *agapē,* was seldom used outside of the Bible. When the Greeks did use it, it meant a love involving a conscious choice. This word lacked the passion of *eros* and the warmth of *philia.*

In the New Testament the word *agapē* is used repeatedly to describe Christian love. *Eros* is not found at all in the New Testament. *Philia* is used at times, but it seems to have been used to mean about the same thing as *agapē.* Why did the early Christians refuse to use *eros* and choose instead to use *agapē?* They did so because *eros* and *agapē* present two contrasting kinds of love. *Eros* always denotes a love that is called forth by the inherent worth of what is loved. The person with *eros* desires to possess and enjoy the object that is loved. By contrast, *agapē* focuses on the subject's love rather than the object's worth or desirability. *Agapē* is a deliberate choosing to care for and help another person for what can be given to the one being loved, not for what can be gained by the one loving.

As we have already noted, this is the striking uniqueness of God's love. This was the kind of love he showed in choosing Israel, in entering into a covenant with them, and in continuing faithful even when Israel was unfaithful. This was the kind of love seen in the life, death, and resurrection of Jesus Christ. The concept of God's *agapē* became the basis for the distinctive love to which God's people are called. The same word is used of God's love for us and of our love for God and others.

The classic exposition of *agapē* is in 1 Corinthians 13. This famous "love chapter" is one of the most popular passages in the Bible. The poetic beauty of the words is surpassed only by the inspiring challenge of the message. Some scholars believe that Paul had composed this hymnlike description of *agapē* as a separate work; then he inserted it at this point in his letter to Corinth. We have no way of knowing about this; however we do know that the chapter, as it now stands, is an integral part of 1 Corinthians.

Paul was seeking to counteract the problem of pride and dissension in the church. In chapters 12—14 he was confronting problems regarding spiritual gifts, especially the misuse of the gift of tongues. Paul urged the Corinthians to give priority to those gifts that benefited others and built up the church. And he challenged them to let *agapē* guide them in using any spiritual gift.

The description of *agapē* in 1 Corinthians shows clearly the distinctive nature of Christian love. The King James Version translates *agapē* as "charity." However, what we mean by "charity" and what Paul meant by *agapē* are two different things. Verse 3 in the King James Version reads: "Though I bestow all my goods to feed the poor . . . and have not *charity*, it profiteth me nothing." To us, bestowing our goods to feed the poor *is* charity. Thus "love" is a better translation than "charity." However, because "love" is ambiguous, we must be careful to note what Paul says. Verses 1-3 show that many activities usually considered worthy, good, even loving activities are worthless if they lack the spirit of *agapē*.

Verses 4-7 are the best description of *agapē* in the New Testament. Paul did not try to define *agapē;* rather he listed a series of its characteristics. Paul described what it is and what it is not. Every facet of *agapē* shows that it focuses on others; it is the opposite of selfishness and pride.

Henry Drummond's exposition of 1 Corinthians 13 is appropriately entitled *The Greatest Thing in the World.* Drummond was only echoing Paul's own use of superlatives. Chapter 13 closes by stressing *agapē* as the ideal state of Christian maturity toward which we should be moving (vv. 8-13). *Agapē* like faith and hope is part of the eternal order; yet, Paul says, of these three "the greatest of these is love" (v. 13). Love is greatest because God himself is love; and when we practice such love, we are reflecting God's very nature.

Christian love is the opposite of the selfish pride that seems so natural for the human race. The problem of egotism in the Corinthian church was but a reflection of the plight of humanity as a whole. Each of us tends to center life around self rather than God and others. The result is that life turns inward and produces an ever-tightening circle of self-centered concerns.

We need to distinguish a healthy regard for self from a destructive selfishness. Jesus seems to have allowed for such a healthy self-love when he said, "Love your neighbor *as yourself.*" This seems to imply that Jesus assumed a normal concern for self as the basis upon which to develop a similar and larger concern encompassing neighbors.

Anders Nygren in his book *Agape and Eros* denies that this was what Jesus meant. He sees any form of self-love as a form of *eros* and alien to everything *agapē* stands for. Nygren writes: "Self-love is man's natural condition, and also the reason for the perversity of his will. Everyone knows how by nature he loves himself. *So,* says the commandment of love, thou shalt love thy neighbour." [2]

While expressing appreciation for the overall value of Nygren's work, many scholars believe that he overstated his case. Paul

E. Johnson notes: "The text does not read, Love thy neighbor *instead* of thyself, but, *As* you love yourself, love *also* your neighbor. Self-love is actually the standard by which to love others. It not only assumes a self-love but even takes it as the measure of neighbor love." [3]

The point is that there is a difference between a sinful selfishness and a healthy concern for oneself. Selfishness is a narrow self-centeredness that closes out God and others except as they can benefit the selfish person. Healthy self-love is the acceptance of oneself as a person made in God's image and loved and accepted by God in spite of sins and imperfections. Thus, self is given the potential for loving God and others.

If we interpret the love command in the light of the Golden Rule of Matthew 7:12, the idea seems to be "Love your neighbor as though he were yourself." That is, put yourself in your neighbor's place; then act in the light of how you would want to be treated if you were your neighbor.

This kind of love involves a radical reorientation of all of life. This was the kind of living called for by Jesus when he called people to deny themselves, take up their crosses, and follow him. Luke's version of this saying (9:23) includes the word "daily." This is what Paul had in mind when he talked about being crucified with Christ (Gal. 2:20). For a Christian, the cross means not only the door to the Christian life but also the pattern and power of the Christian life. We become saved sinners as we receive God's love revealed through the cross. Then we are called to practice the same kind of love that God has shown to us. "For the love of Christ controls us, because we are convinced that one has died for all; therefore all have died. And he died for all, that those who live might live no longer for themselves but for him who for their sake died and was raised" (2 Cor. 5:14-15).

This radical reorientation of life does not mean that Christians love with perfect *agapē*. Only God's *agapē* is perfect; ours is at best a dim reflection of his. However, God's *agapē* in our lives does give us a potential not before possessed. His love transforms all our loves. *Eros* and *philia* are still valid kinds of love, but they are now shaped and tempered by *agapē*.

C. S. Lewis has an intriguing study of Christian love entitled *The Four Loves*. He distinguishes Gift-love and Need-love. Gift-love is the self-giving love like God's love for us—based solely on the love of the giver, not on the lovableness of the one loved. Need-love is a love based on the need to be loved. Lewis says that God transforms and makes possible each of these kinds of love in Christian experience. We respond to God and to others with both kinds of love. We respond with Need-love to God when we swallow our pride and accept his grace for us— something based solely on God's love, not on our own goodness and lovableness. We respond with Gift-love to God as we give ourselves completely to him. We respond with Gift-love to others when we act on their behalf with no thought of receiving anything except the privilege of giving love. We respond with Need-love to others when we can accept someone else's Gift-love toward us. In other words, we are enabled to give love to God and others and to receive love from God and others in all of life's varied relationships.

Who Is My Neighbor?

George Washington Carver was born a slave. When he was an infant, he and his mother were stolen by night riders. A man named John Bentley was hired to try to bring them back. Days later Bentley came back with the tiny black infant who was more dead than alive. Bentley explained that he had been unable to overtake the raiders. When he was asked where he had found the baby, he replied: "Oh, him. They just give him to some womenfolk down by Conway. He ain't worth nothin'." [4]

This has often been one person's estimate of another person, but no one who accepts the New Testament revelation of God's love can rest easy with such an estimate. God's self-giving love is extended to all people—regardless of who they are or regardless of their potential. We know how wrong Bentley was about that sickly, helpless infant; for we know the valuable contributions made to humanity by George Washington Carver. But God's love for the infant was *not* based on what he would later accomplish in life; God's love was based on God's nature to love. This kind of love cares for people regardless of what they have been, of what they become, or of what they are.

Jesus first told the parable of the good Samaritan to a lawyer who had asked this question: "Who is my neighbor?" (Luke 10:29). The lawyer had correctly noted the importance of the two great love commandments (vv. 25-28), but he apparently was not willing to accept as neighbors all those whom Jesus considered to be neighbors. The way he phrased his question shows that he was anxious to restrict the category of "neighbor" in some way. He wanted to be able to leave some people out of the circle of his concern.

The parable strongly challenges this view. Nothing is said about the injured man's nationality, vocation, economic or social status; he is simply called *a man*—an injured man. Jesus made the hero of the story a Samaritan. The hard feelings between Jews and Samaritans was a fact of life in those days. A Samaritan was an unlikely hero for a story to a Jewish audience, but Jesus had a reason for making the Samaritan the hero. A Jewish priest and a Levite passed by the injured man, but the Samaritan stopped and helped him. He did not do this because the injured man was a Samaritan or because he was a Jew but because he was a human being.

Thus Jesus defined "neighbor" as a fellow human being—white, black, rich, poor, Christian, non-Christian. God has created all people in his image, and his love includes all. Every person is loved by God, thus potentially a child of God. Christ died for all.

In Matthew 5:43-47 Jesus interpreted "neighbor" to include enemies. He rebuked those who had defined love for neighbor in such a way that they could continue to hate their enemies. He commanded his followers to love their enemies. He based this command on the fact that God loves all people. The Father sends the blessings of sunshine and rain to all men; this is a sign of his love for all. Those who are recognized as God's sons show the same kind of self-giving, impartial love. Anything less falls short of Christian love. All men—believers and nonbelievers—love those who love them. This kind of love is natural. Thus Jesus calls his followers to love as God does—to love those who do not love us, to love those who hate us and do us harm.

Christian love should extend to *neighbors* and *enemies,* but it should begin with *brothers.* This last word is used particularly in John's writings: "This commandment we have from him, that he who loves God love his brother also" (1 John 4:21). At the Last Supper, Jesus said: "A new commandment I give to you, that you love one another; even as I have loved you, that you also love one another. By this all men will know that you are my disciples, if you have love for one another" (John 13:34-35). If Christians cannot love one another, how shall we ever be able to love our enemies? Our relationships with those who share our faith should be the training ground for developing our capacity to love those who do not share our faith.

The motivating power for such love is the love God has shown us in Christ. Writing to Christians, Paul said, "Walk in love, as Christ loved us and gave himself up for us" (Eph. 5:2). As already noted, 1 Corinthians 13 was an appeal addressed to a congregation that desperately needed to practice love toward one another. Something of the same disruptive spirit, though on a smaller scale, was at work in the Philippian congregation (Phil. 2:14; 4:2). Paul wanted to head this off before it became more serious; therefore, he appealed to them to show the same kind of love for one another that was seen in the self-giving love of Jesus Christ (2:1-8).

The word "brother" points to the church as a family of faith and love, bound together by ties of love from and to God our Father. Loving our brothers is sometimes little easier than loving those outside the family. God has a way of loving and accepting all kinds of people. (After all, he loved and accepted us!) All the same potential for interpersonal conflicts, rivalries, misunderstandings as exist anywhere exist in a church. Therefore, we constantly need to reaffirm our love for God and one another.

Suppose you are an orphaned child, and a kind, generous man adopts you. He makes you his child, brings you to his house, and shares his bounty with you. But this bighearted benefactor has a way of befriending and adopting other orphans. Soon you discover that you are one of many children who call this man "father." Very likely you will experience some difficulties in getting along with all the others. One fact, however, should help you and them seek to get along—the realization that the man who loves you also loves all the others. Hopefully this should help all of you think of one another as brothers because of the love all of you have received from and feel toward your father. This is a parable of how Christian brothers should be bound together by the love of the heavenly Father.

Christian love should begin even closer to home—in the home itself. The New Testament uses the word *agapē* to refer to the kind of love that a husband shows to his wife: "Husbands, love your wives, as Christ loved the church and gave himself up for her (Eph. 5:25). Love in a Christian marriage should involve *eros, philia,* and *agapē.* No two people should consider marriage unless they are deeply in love in every sense of the term. They should have deep feelings of affection and attraction for one another. They should want and need each other. Yet undergirding and tempering all of the natural feelings of married love should be the kind of self-giving love that gives priority to the needs of the other person.

Many ministers use 1 Corinthians 13 as a part of the wedding ceremony. Although the passage was not directed originally to married couples as such, the contents of the chapter apply to Christian love within marriage. The first three verses, for example, may be paraphrased to fit the marriage relationship:

> If a groom and a bride speak with the language of persons passionately in love, but have not *agapē*, their words will be drowned out by the winds of passing time and circumstance. And if a couple is well-favored with good looks and good health, and if they have a strong physical attraction for one another, but have not *agapē*, they may someday wonder if they really love one another anymore. And even if they are completely compatible in every way, enjoy one another's company, and have every promise of a happy life together, but have not *agapē*, they lack what they need most for a happy, enduring marriage.

Love Is Something You Do

A young minister was talking with a Christian lady who was a member of his congregation and a good friend. The conversation had turned to the subject of a man who had caused trouble for both of them. The minister had spoken some hard words about their mutual antagonist; then feeling a little guilty he said: "But there I go! There you have it! How in heaven's name, as Christians are we supposed to love a man like that?"

His friend replied: "You sound as if you expected yourself to be able to be fond of him. But that's nonsense, isn't it? I don't believe Jesus Christ is interested in nonsense. Fondness, affection for people can be cultivated, but it cannot at will be turned on or off like a faucet. Christian love must be something other than that. I'm fairly certain Christ understands that *if I'm required to love that man, it must be as a principle, not as an emotion!*" [5]

Those words of wisdom helped the minister, Frederick Speakman, realize that Christian love begins with action, not emotion. This love begins with *something we do,* not with something we feel. This insight first crashed into my consciousness when I read the following words written by C. S. Lewis: "Do not waste time bothering whether you 'love' your neighbour; act as if you did. As soon as we do this we find one of the great secrets. When you are behaving as if you loved someone, you will presently come to love him." [6]

The way Lewis stated this shocked me. My initial impulse was to argue with him: "Would it not be hypocritical to act toward a person as if I love him when actually I do not?" But the more I reflected on this, the more sense Lewis made. I realized that if I wait until I love some people before I act kindly toward them, I will be waiting a long time. A closer reading of Lewis showed that he distinguished between *liking* a person and *doing good* to a person. Christian love does not necessarily mean liking a person; rather it means doing good to a person.

How else can we love our *enemies?* The very fact that they are our enemies means that bad feelings are involved. When Jesus said that we were to love our enemies, he did not mean that we are to strain for all we can and see if we can come up with feelings of fondness and affection for our enemies. He meant that we should do good to our enemies however we may feel about them. Our natural impulse is to get back at someone who has hurt us. Jesus said that instead of striking back we should do good to our enemy (Matt. 5:38-47). Paul doubtlessly had the words of Jesus in mind when he wrote Romans 12:17-21: In verse 20 Paul quoted Proverbs 25:21-22: "If your enemy is hungry, feed him; if he is thirsty, give him drink; for by so doing you will be heaping burning coals upon his head."

As Lewis notes, sometimes as we pray for an enemy and do good to him, our feelings toward him change. Sometimes the enemy himself changes. Perhaps this is what Paul meant by heaping coals of fire on his head: sometimes acts of love cause an enemy to soften and to change. However, this is not always true. Sometimes the enemy only becomes more cruel and hateful.

But in any case, the Christian's responsibility is to do him good.

How else can we love the unnumbered multitude of all kinds of people whom Jesus would have us call our *neighbors?* Should we spend our time trying to work up warm feelings for all humanity? If it were possible, what purpose would it serve? Many people love everyone in general but no one in particular. The test of Christian love for our neighbors is how we treat them, not how we feel about them. How do you suppose the Samaritan *felt* when he saw the injured man lying alongside the road? He probably felt fear that the robbers might be using the man as bait to lure another victim. He may have felt a little sick as he looked at the man's wounds. He probably felt pity for the man's plight. Did not the priest and Levite also have these same feelings? The difference was not in their feelings but in their actions. The Samaritan went to the man, dressed his wounds, put him on his animal, carried him to an inn, and took care of him. Then when the Samaritan left, he gave the innkeeper some extra money and promised to pay the man's other expenses when he returned. Thus when Jesus asked which of the three travelers proved to be a neighbor, the lawyer could only reply, "The one who showed mercy on him" (Luke 10:37).

Recall the parable in Matthew 25:31-46. For what was one group condemned and the other group commended? Jesus did not say: "When I was hungry, you felt sorry for me; when I was thirsty, you were so concerned; when I was sick, you felt very sympathetic." Instead he spoke of actions: *fed, gave drink, welcomed, clothed, visited.*

The same principle holds true of love for our brothers in Christ: the test of love is always actions. First John 3:16-18 says it well:

> By this we know love, that he laid down his life for us; and we ought to lay down our lives for the brethren. But if anyone has the world's goods and sees his brother in need, yet closes his heart against him, how does God's love abide in him? Little

children, let us not love in word or speech but in deed and in truth.

Ernest Gordon's book *Through the Valley of the Kwai* is an amazing story of Christian love in action. Gordon spent three and one-half years in Japanese POW camps during World War II. Early in their imprisonment many of the men turned to religion expecting God to come quickly to their aid. As time passed, however, they turned away from religion feeling that God had let them down. The treatment by their captors was indescribably brutal. The Japanese set out to break the proud Westerners, and they succeeded in doing this. The prisoners practiced a law-of-the-jungle kind of existence: They fought over scraps of food; they stole from one another; they ignored the weak, the sick, the dying, the dead.

Then the actions of a few began to change the attitude of the whole camp. In Gordon's case, two men nursed him back from the brink of the grave. Another man literally starved himself to death trying to keep a sick buddy alive. Another prisoner stepped forward to take undeserved execution rather than see the whole work detail executed. The concern of these few was contagious. Others began to reach out to help one another. They helped the weak, tended the sick, comforted the dying, and reverently buried their dead. They shared with one another what they had. As they did, they were being reborn to new life. Gordon recalls:

> It was dawning on us all—officers and "other ranks" alike—that the law of the jungle is not for men. We had seen for ourselves how quickly it could strip us of our humanity and reduce us to levels lower than the beasts.
>
> Death was still with us—no doubt about that. But we were being slowly freed from its destructive grip. We were seeing for ourselves the sharp contrasts between the forces that make for life and those that make for death. Selfishness, hatred, jealousy, greed were all anti-life. Love, self-sacrifice, mercy, and creative

faith, on the other hand, were the essence of life, turning mere existence into living in its truest sense. These were the gifts of God to men. [7]

The prisoners even found opportunities of doing good to their enemies. They gave food and drink to some wounded Japanese soldiers who were being ignored by their own countrymen. When the Allied troops arrived after the Japanese surrendered, they wanted to kill the prison guards for what they had done. Only the restraint of the prisoners kept the Allied soldiers from this act of vengeance.

This kind of love is costly. During the years of captivity, some of the Christians were killed by guards who were infuriated by their attempts to show love. One of the men who had nursed Ernest Gordon back to health was a quiet-spoken young Christian. A Japanese officer hated him so much for his goodness that he literally crucified the young Christian on a tree.

Christian love is always a risky venture. The person who reaches out to help someone exposes himself to being hurt. His love may be misunderstood, ignored, rejected—even violently rejected. But what is the alternative? It too is costly—but in a different way. Love is risky, but lovelessness is more costly because it is deadly.

> To love at all is to be vulnerable. Love anything, and your heart will certainly be wrung and possibly be broken. If you want to make sure of keeping it intact, you must give your heart to no one. . . . Wrap it carefully round with hobbies and little luxuries; avoid all entanglements; lock it up safe in the casket or coffin of your selfishness. But in that casket—safe, dark, motionless, airless—it will change. It will not be broken; it will become unbreakable, impenetrable, irredeemable. [8]

Summary

1. Our ability to love is based on our trust in a God who loves us.

2. The test of our professed love for God is our practiced love toward others.

3. Christian love turns life inside out by turning us from self-centered living to a life centered in the will of God and the needs of others.

4. The circle of Christian love includes all people, including our enemies; and the practice of Christian love should begin in the church and in the home.

5. Christian love is doing good for the other person, irregardless of our feelings for the person.

---

[1] A. Leonard Griffith, *Beneath the Cross of Jesus* (Nashville: Abingdon Press, 1961), p. 14.

[2] Anders Nygren, *Agape and Eros,* translated by Philip S. Watson (Philadelphia: The Westminster Press, 1953), p. 101.

[3] Paul E. Johnson, *Christian Love* (Nashville: Abingdon-Cokesbury Press, 1951), p. 39.

[4] Lawrence Elliott, *George Washington Carver: The Man Who Overcame* (Englewood Cliffs, N.J.: Prentice-Hall, Inc. 1966), p. 14.

[5] Frederick B. Speakman, *Love Is Something You Do* (Westwood, N.J.: Fleming H. Revell Co., 1959), pp. 13-14.

[6] C. S. Lewis, *Mere Christianity* (New York: The Macmillan Company, 1958), p. 101.

[7] Ernest Gordon, *Through the Valley of the Kwai* (New York: Harper & Bros., 1962), pp. 108-109.

[8] C. S. Lewis, *The Four Loves* (New York: Harcourt, Brace & World, Inc., 1960), p. 169.

hope —what keeps us going 3

Ethel Rogers Mulvaney was a Red Cross worker captured by the Japanese when Singapore fell in 1942. She was one of four thousand people crowded into a jail designed to accommodate four hundred and fifty prisoners. The terrible conditions bred feelings of hopelessness among the prisoners.

As Easter approached, Mrs. Mulvaney went to the Japanese prison commandant and asked permission to sing hymns on Easter morning. The commandant refused. The dauntless Red Cross worker was persistent; she went back time and time again. Finally the commandant told her that the women prisoners could sing for five minutes in the prison courtyard. When Easter came, the women assembled and sang the songs of praise and hope based on Christ's resurrection. As they sang, a lone Japanese soldier stood guard. As the prisoners marched silently back to their quarters, the Japanese guard stepped up to Mrs. Mulvaney. He drew out a tiny orchid from under his shirt and handed it to her. As he did, he whispered these words: "Christ *did* rise!" [1]

This is a true parable of Christian hope in a troubled world. The dark plight of the world makes for despair, but the message of Christian hope pierces through the darkness. This hope, based on Christ's resurrection, gives us the courage to go on.

"Hope" is what Carl Sandburg called a "homespun word." This ordinary, garden-variety word represents a reality that is a part of human life. All languages are filled with sayings that speak of hope in this way. Alexander Pope wrote, "Hope springs eternal in the human breast." One of our most famous English proverbs is: "Where there's life, there's hope."

Psychiatrist Karl Menninger prefers to turn the saying around to read "Where there's hope, there's life." This saying emphasizes that human life is enriched and sustained by hope. Menninger believes that from a purely scientific point of view human hope is essential for life and health.

"Hope"—like "life" and "love"—is another four-letter word found repeatedly in the Bible. This is not surprising. Since the Bible is a chronicle of human life and destiny, a reader would naturally expect to read much of man's hopes and dreams. However, the way the Bible uses the word "hope" is distinctive. At times the Bible does use "hope" in the same way that "hope" is used in ordinary, everyday conversation. For example, Paul wrote of the plowman and the thresher working in "hope" of sharing in the harvest (1 Cor. 9:10). However, most of the biblical references to "hope" have a meaning somewhat different from what most people mean when they use the word. In a sense, this ordinary word has been baptized into Christ and filled with new meaning and significance.

Blessing or Curse?

The Greek myth of Pandora's box gives an ancient version of the origin of hope. According to the story, Zeus created Pandora with a malicious purpose in mind. Zeus was angry because Prometheus had stolen fire from the gods and given it to humanity. Because of a law among the gods and goddesses on Mount Olympus, a god could not take back any gift given to man. Therefore, Zeus planned a way to give an evil gift that would counterbalance the good gift of fire. Having created Pandora (which means All-gifted), Zeus gave her a beautiful box. Unknown to her, Zeus had filled the box with all kinds of evils and troubles. Epimetheus, Pandora's husband, was suspicious of Zeus' gift; therefore, he warned Pandora not to open the box. Pandora promised not to open it, but eventually her curiosity got the best of her. She cracked the lid slightly in order to peek in. As she did, a swarm of evils rushed out and scattered among mankind. Because of her curiosity, she had let loose on hapless mortals the cares, woes, and diseases that afflict mankind. At first she thought the box was now empty, but she discovered that one thing remained inside—hope.

There are many versions of this ancient myth. In many of these, hope is seen as a blessing, remaining to comfort and console a mortal race afflicted by all manner of evils. However, in the ancient Greek version of the story, hope is looked on as no less evil than the other evils that escaped from the box. Many Greek writers had this cynical view of hope. They labeled hope as a two-faced deceiver who causes men to strive eagerly for the unattainable, while all the time age, disease, and death overtake them. They claimed that hope is a deceitful goddess luring men on with dreams that turn into nightmares.

The same mixed reviews of hope are found in the literature of most people. Many in every generation agree with the ancient Greek version of Pandora. An old English proverb says, "Hope is a good breakfast but a bad supper." Another proverb is, "He who lives on hope will die fasting." Still another says, "He who lives in hope dances without music." Abraham Cowley wrote, "Hope is the most hopeless thing of all." The brooding German philosopher Nietzsche wrote, "Hope is the worst of all evils, for it prolongs the torment of man." The sharp-tongued journalist H. L. Mencken delivered this verbal salvo: "Hope is the pathological belief in the occurrence of the impossible."

Why this cynicism about hope? Is hope a blessing or is it a curse? In order to answer these questions, we need to clearly define the meaning of "hope." The Greek word for hope is *elpis*. Both words—"hope" and *elpis*—have two elements: desire and expectation. In colloquial English usage, however, the element of desire often outweighs the element of expectation. Hope then becomes little more than wishful thinking. When a person says, "I hope so," he often means little more than "I wish it were so."

Cynics assume that all hope is in this category of being little more than wishful thinking. Therefore, in the name of realism they deny that hope has any positive value; in fact, they charge that hope is harmful. The mistake of the cynics is that they have lumped together all kinds of hopes. They have failed to distinguish between real hope and counterfeit hopes. The fact that hope is little more than wishful thinking for some people does not mean that all hope is illusory.

"Hope" as used in the Bible is more than wishful thinking. In fact the Bible adds a third element to the meaning of hope—confidence. This is because the emphasis in the Bible is not only what hope we hope *for* but also what we hope *in*. The Hebrew words for "hope" in the Old Testament emphasize not only the idea of patient waiting for a desired expectation but also the idea of firm confidence in the God of hope who will bring this to pass. The Greeks spoke of what they hoped *for;* the Hebrews spoke of whom they hoped *in*—they placed their hope in God. Jeremiah referred to God as "the hope of Israel" (14:8; 17:13). Psalm 71:5 says: "For thou, O Lord, are my hope, my trust, O Lord, from my youth." The writer of Psalms 42–43 (which were originally one psalm) recounted his despair as he passed through times of difficulty and depression. Three times (42:5,11; 43:5) he called himself to renewed hope with these words:

> Why are you cast down, O my soul,
>   and why are you disquieted within me?
> Hope in God; for I shall again praise him,
>   my help and my God.

This note of confident hope is also characteristic of the New

Testament. "We have our hope set on the living God, who is the Savior of all men" (1 Tim. 4:10). Paul told Timothy to charge the rich "not to be haughty, nor to set their hopes on uncertain riches but on God who richly furnishes us with everything to enjoy" (1 Tim. 6:17). From the Christian perspective, we also can speak of Christ Jesus as "our hope" (1 Tim. 1:1).

The Bible sees God as the only adequate foundation for hope. When Paul was writing to Gentile converts, he gave this description of their former condition before coming to Christ: "Remember that you were at that time separated from Christ, alienated from the commonwealth of Israel, and strangers to the covenants of promise, having no hope and without God in the world" (Eph. 2:12). Paul, of course, was not denying that they had had many hopes prior to their new relation to God; however he was saying that they had had no real basis for hope so long as they were "without God."

Cynicism and despair are marks of our age. One man expressed his hopelessness in these words: "We are alone in a terrifying and uncaring universe." Such despair is a direct result of an absence of any faith in God. Those who have no faith in the God of hope are doomed either to hopelessness or to false hopes.

Samuel Beckett's play *Waiting for Godot* is an important work in what has come to be called the theater of the absurd. Beckett is one of the writers who vividly and sometimes shockingly portrays the emptiness and absurdity of human existence. *Waiting for Godot* focuses on two old tramps who are waiting for the arrival of someone called Godot. They seem to know little about Godot other than that they are supposed to keep waiting for him.

Each of the two acts of the play covers one day of empty waiting. On each day a boy claiming to be from Godot comes to tell the two tramps that Godot will not be coming on that day but surely on the next day. The waiting is aimless and monotonous; and increasingly the audience comes to feel it is utterly hopeless. The action—or, to be more exact, the lack of action—of the second day is an almost exact duplication of the first day. Each day closes with one man saying to the other, "Well, shall we go?" The other replies, "Yes, let's go." [2] But neither moves. They seem doomed to wait forever—for nothing.

Waiting for Godot is a vivid parable of the hopelessness of human existence. Many viewers and readers conclude that Godot represents the God whom many await but who never comes to our aid. To many moderns God is surely absent, and he is probably nonexistent. And without God, human life is reduced to a wasteland of despair—without meaning, without purpose, without hope.

God's Hope and Man's Hopes

Even when people today speak of faith and hope, they often do so with little or no reference to faith or hope *in God.* A famous man was once asked what he believed in. He replied, "I believe in myself—with fingers crossed." He was honest enough to confess both the real basis for his faith and his uneasiness about it. This is an apt summary of our age: "We believe in ourselves with fingers crossed." We do not really believe in God but in ourselves; however in our more thoughtful moments we are aware how unsubstantial is the foundation for our faith and hope.

What a contrast is that person whose hope and trust is in God! One of Martin Luther's enemies once tried to shake him by sneering: "Tell me, when the whole world turns against you—church, state, princes, people—where will you be then?" Luther replied, "Why, then as now, I will be in the hands of Almighty God."

This is what it means to make God your hope. A person whose hope is based on anything other than God is building on shifting sands. A person whose hope is in God is building on a firm and lasting foundation. This kind of hope survives all the storms of changing circumstances.

The Bible uses several ways of referring to this kind of hope. As we have seen, the Bible often speaks of putting our *hope in God,* and it sometimes speaks of *God* as *our hope.* The Bible also speaks of *the God of hope.* This title is found in Romans 15:13, a benediction prayer: "May the God of hope fill you with all joy and peace in believing, so that by the power of the Holy Spirit you may abound in hope."

God himself is the basis for and the source of Christian hope. Implicit in all these expressions is the idea that God himself is *the God who hopes.* As the God of hope, he can give us hope because of his own hope.

In Ephesians 1:18 Paul prayed that his readers might better know God and "the hope of his calling." The King James Version gives the literal rendering of the language, thus leaving the reader to decide what Paul meant. The Revised Standard Version interprets "the hope of his calling" to mean "the hope to which he has called you." This is one possible meaning. However, another strong possibility is that "the hope of his calling" refers to the hope God has in calling men to himself. This "hope" of God is the basis of the hope to which he calls us. He calls us to share with him in his hope or purpose.

W. O. Carver wrote an excellent study of Ephesians, *The Glory of God in the Christian Calling.* Carver strongly defended this interpretation of "the hope of his calling" in Ephesians 1:18: "This is to be understood of God's hope in calling us, not what we may hope for in that he has called us." [3] Critics of this view maintain that God is incapable of hope since he already has all knowledge, but Carver points out that the Bible often attributes human traits to God in order to communicate what God is like. God does not hope in the sense that men do when they gaze off into an uncertain future and hope. However, God does hope in the sense that he has a desired plan and purpose toward which he is moving history and toward which he summons us to join him.

In Ephesians 4:4 Paul spoke of the unifying force of God's hope when he reminded his readers, "Ye were called in one hope of your calling." Once again the Revised Standard Version interprets this to mean, "You were called to the one hope that belongs to your call." This interpretation is not incorrect, but it fails to stress the divine source of the calling and the hope. The calling and the hope belong to God, but when one enters into that calling and hope, it becomes his also. Thus Christian hope is the one hope that all the called ones share with the God who called us.

Understanding this concept is absolutely essential in understanding Christian hope. When we speak of ourselves as people whose hope is in God, we are not saying that we believe that God will make all our hopes become realities. What we mean is that we believe that God's kingdom shall come and his will shall be done.

What then is the relationship between this one divine-human hope and the ordinary hopes of humanity?

1. *Many human hopes are disqualified as unworthy by comparison with Christian hope.*—The book of Acts, for example, tells of the owners of a slave girl who were angered at Paul when he healed her of a spirit of divination. They were angry because her healing had taken away "their hope of gain" (16:19). Similarly, Felix kept Paul in prison even though he knew Paul was innocent. The Roman procurator did this because "he hoped that money would be given him by Paul" (24:26).

Such selfish hopes have nothing at all to do with Christian hope. In fact, they represent all that is contradictory to Christian hope.

2. *No Christian can expect God to guarantee all his individual hopes.*—As human beings, Christians have all or most of the ordinary hopes that other people have. We hope for good health,

long life, success, and so forth. Such hopes are normal and right. However, some people make the mistake of assuming that because they are Christians, all their dreams should come true. Such people often react with shock when their fondest hopes do not materialize. They sometimes react with bitterness and self-pity when some of their dreams become nightmares. One such woman recounted a series of recent troubles, then she said: "We have always been religious people. We have gone to church faithfully, and now this has happened. How can we believe in God anymore?"

The Bible never promises that our hopes will all come true and that we will be spared trouble and pain. To the contrary, we are told to expect disappointments and troubles. However, the wonderful thing about sharing in God's hope is that this hope cannot fail. Troubles do not destroy it. In fact, paradoxically, trials often make this hope brighter and stronger because trials have a way of forcing us to fall back on what is real and enduring (Rom. 5:1-5).

3. *Christian hope shapes and determines many of the hopes of Christians.*—Although God does not guarantee to fulfill all our hopes, he is concerned about all our hopes; and increasingly our hopes are permeated by the one hope we share with God. For example, Paul often wrote about his plans to travel from one place to another in his missionary work. For instance, he wrote to the Romans: "I hope to see you in passing as I go to Spain, and to be sped on my journey there by you, once I have enjoyed your company for a little" (Rom. 15:24; see also 1 Cor. 16:7; Phil. 2:23; 1 Tim. 3:14). Such travel plans were shaped by Paul's commitment to the Christian hope. His hope to visit Rome and Spain was a part of his commitment as a missionary. Thus Paul had more than ordinary confidence in these hopes.

However, Paul knew that he was not God. His knowledge of God's will was not perfect. At the time, his hope to go to

Rome and then to Spain seemed to him to be the Lord's will. Later Paul did go to Rome, but he went not as a traveler but as a prisoner. Thus, God worked out his own plan in his own way. Paul did not fret because of this; he did not feel that his hopes had been dashed. Rather he rejoiced that God was using him to work out the divine plan as it seemed best to God.

4. *Thus the one hope in which Christians have absolute confidence is God's hope.*—Although many of our hopes are so permeated by God's hope that they become almost expressions of it, only the hope that begins and ends with God can bear the full weight of our confidence and trust. This hope is as sure and certain as God himself.

Romans 4:18 is a striking example of a man who held to this hope in the face of seemingly insurmountable obstacles. Paul was describing Abraham's hope of an heir when he wrote, "In hope he believed against hope." From this paradoxical statement we got our expression "hoping against hope." Abraham continued to have hope even when the situation seemed hopeless. Although from a human point of view he had absolutely no basis for hope, he continued to hope in God. He hoped in God because of God's purpose related to God's own redemptive purpose and plan.

Hope and Death

Rodin's *The First Funeral* captures man's feelings about the mystery of death. The sculptor has reproduced in a striking way the emotions of the first humans to confront death. This work of art shows the sculptured figures of Adam and Eve as they view the dead body of their son Abel. Eve is distracted with her grief. Adam looks down in sorrow and bewilderment at the limp form in his arms. Men have stood in awe and fear before death ever since. What does Christian hope say about death?

Nearly all ancient societies had some concept of survival after death. In most cases this was more an assumption from the nature of things than a religious hope. The ancient Greeks had such a view. They believed that people continued to exist in a vague, shadowy region beyond death; but this existence was not an enviable one at all. Thus the Greeks of Homer's stories viewed death with resignation but not with hope.

The ancient Hebrew view was similar. The shadowy region beyond death was called *sheol,* but this existence was far short of anything that might be called life. Thus the general Old Testament view stresses earthly hopes, not hopes of life after death. There was a feeling of skepticism about the value of existence in *sheol.* The author of Ecclesiastes expressed the outlook of many in Israel when he wrote, "He who is joined with all the living has hope, for a living dog is better than a dead lion" (Eccl. 9:4). In other words, however illusory earthly life may be, it is far better than any sort of existence in *sheol.* Righteous King Hezekiah, after his recovery from an illness that nearly proved fatal, praised God with these words (Isa. 38:18):

> For Sheol cannot thank thee,
>   death cannot praise thee;
> those who go down to the pit cannot hope
>   for thy faithfulness.

Toward the end of the Old Testament period, a few in Israel began to probe the possibility of life after death. For example, at points in his spiritual pilgrimage, Job expressed such a hope. He had assumed the traditional view that excluded such a hope. However, Job's predicament drove him to reexamine some of his traditional beliefs. His faith in God's justice led him tentatively to a view that expects an afterlife in which earthly injustices will be righted by God.

The tone of the New Testament is strikingly different from the Old Testament on the subject of life after death. At best the Old Testament suggests this as a possibility, but the New

Testament declares this as a confident hope. There is nothing tentative about these ringing words in 1 Peter 1:3: "Blessed be the God and Father of our Lord Jesus Christ! By his great mercy we have been born anew to a living hope through the resurrection of Jesus Christ from the dead."

This "living hope" is not based on tentative assumptions about the nature of things; it is based on the resurrection of Jesus Christ. His victory over death is the basis for our hope of victory over death. In 1 Corinthians 15 Paul spelled this out. In verses 12-19 he dared his readers to face the alternatives to faith in Christ's resurrection. If Christ has not been raised from the dead, everything we believe and hope for is an illusion. Verse 19 says, "If we have only hoped in Christ in this life, we are of all men most pitiable" (ASV). Paul's point was that if Christ is not risen, there is no real basis for Christian hope; believers have only hoped as unbelievers hope—with no real basis for our hope. Such empty hoping, if it were true, would make Christians pitiful indeed, for our hope would then never be fulfilled. Paul used this approach in order to stress how crucial the resurrection of Christ is for Christian hope.

One of Paul's purposes in writing to the Thessalonians was to deal with their concern about their loved ones who had died in Christ. Paul told his readers that he was writing so that they might not "grieve as others who have no hope" (1 Thess. 4:13). Paul did not mean that Christians should not pass through the feelings of grief that are normal for all people who lose loved ones. However, he did mean that the Christian's grief is not the hopeless despair that characterizes unbelievers.

The inscriptions on the tombs of the period just before Christ are almost completely devoid of any hope of life after death. The contrast between these expressions of despair and the epitaphs on the tombs of early Christians is striking indeed. The ancient world was hungry for the message of hope proclaimed by the followers of Christ. Christianity did not win the ancient world by presenting a superior morality (although its morality was superior) but by proclaiming a victory over death.

Tragically many people today—even those in lands with a Christian heritage—no longer believe in life after death. This is not surprising: a generation that has lost its faith in God can hardly be expected to maintain its hope of heaven. Many people have lost their grip on the Christian hope—at least as the early Christians understood it.

The modern approach to death is denial, not hope. Modern man has done everything possible to avoid and evade the subject of death. Many have even gone so far as to claim that death is irrelevant: modern man is interested in this life, not in what happens after death.

Death is a very personal thing. Dying is something each must face—and face alone. All the bravado is well enough until I am the one who is staring death in the face. Then death becomes intensely personal, very relevant—all in fact that counts.

The play *The Best Man* contains a poignant scene about facing death. Two politicians are discussing God, religion, and the hereafter. Both men admit that they believe neither in God nor in life after death. One of the men, an old veteran politician, confides to his younger friend that he is dying of cancer; the doctor has given him only a few months to live. The younger man is shocked and deeply concerned about his friend, but he cannot find anything reassuring to say. Finally he says: "But there's hope in this: Every act we make sets off a chain of reaction which never ends. And if we are reasonably . . . good, well, there *is* some consolation in that, a kind of immortality." The old politician replies dryly: "I suggest you tell yourself that when *you* finally have to face a whole pile of nothin' up ahead." [4]

How tragic to face death with no hope! For that matter, how tragic to face life without hope. A person is prepared neither to live nor to die until he is firmly grounded in the Christian hope.

What a contrast between the hopelessness of the old politician and the hope of a committed Christian. My friend D. P. Brooks tells of his father's hope in the face of death: "To him dying was not a passing into nothingness. Beyond death was the One who had never failed him in a long life, and he dared to believe that neither death nor life could separate him from Christ." [5]

Immortality or Resurrection?

Benjamin Franklin wrote his own epitaph:

> The Body of Benjamin Franklin Printer,
> Like the Covering of an old Book,
> Its Contents torn out,
> And script of its Lettering and Gilding,
> Lies here, Food for Worms;
> But the Work shall not be lost,
> It will (as he believed) appear once more,
> In a new and more beautiful Edition,
> Corrected and amended
> By the Author.

Franklin's epitaph comes close to expressing the biblical view of life beyond death. The Christian hope of life after death is a hope of resurrection. The resurrection will not be a literal raising of the flesh-and-blood body, but God will give us a new body fit for our new mode of existence.

First Corinthians 15 is the classic description of this hope. Paul was writing to counteract the teaching that "there is no resurrection of the dead" (v. 12). Some of the members of the Corinthian church were probably teaching the immortality of the soul but denying the resurrection of the body. Most of the Greeks had no hope of any kind, but some did have a hope of life after death. However, they defined their hope as the immortality of the soul, not the resurrection of the body. Several centuries before Christ the Greek philosopher Plato taught that the soul of man is immortal. Some of the Greek mystery religions also taught that after death the immortal soul escapes the corruptible body, which has been its prison during life. On one thing all the Greeks agreed—there can be no resurrection of the body.

Very possibly, some of the Corinthians were interpreting the Christian hope in such a way as to deny resurrection. Paul insisted that the Christian hope is resurrection, not immortality. He said that the resurrection of Jesus points to a future resurrection of believers; denying one is denying the other. When Paul described the nature of the resurrection body, he made two important points: (1) It is not the same flesh-and-blood mortal body that is buried; (2) On the other hand, it is a body, a spiritual body. This may sound like double-talk, but Paul was seeking to preserve an important truth.

Most people today who have any hope of life after death define their hope in terms of immortality, not resurrection. This is true even of many Christians; we are often closer to Plato than to Paul. This is unfortunate because the resurrection hope is the biblical hope of life after death. Most people shy away from the resurrection hope because they think it means a resuscitation of the mortal body. As we have noted, this is not what it means. What then does it mean? What are the real distinctions between the biblical hope of resurrection and the Greek hope of immortality?

1. *Immortality is based on the nature of man; resurrection is based on the power of God.* Immortality is an assumption from the nature of things. Philosophers look at man and decide that a creature with such potential cannot be snuffed out at death. There must be an immortal part of man that lives on, even beyond death. So they conclude that although man's body perishes, man has a soul that is immortal. Christians who believe in immortality would say that man's soul is immortal because this is how God made him. However, not everyone who believes in immortality believes in God. As we noted in chapter 1, even

an atheist can believe that man is inherently immortal.

By contrast, resurrection is based not on the nature of man but on the power of God. No one believes in resurrection unless he believes in a God who can raise the dead. Resurrection runs counter to man's makeup. Man is a sinner, and he is mortal. From this hopeless and helpless plight only God can set him free.

Ezekiel 37 is one of the Old Testament passages back of the concept of resurrection. The vision of the making alive of the dry bones referred to Israel's restoration from the "death" of their exiled condition. However, the analogy also applies to the resurrection from the dead. The valley of dry bones gives the biblical view of the human plight. Man is hopelessly under the dominion of death. The bones say, "Our bones are dried up, and our hope is lost; we are clean cut off" (Ezek. 37:11). Their only hope is the miracle-working power of God who makes the dead come alive again.

The New Testament makes this explicit. Death is not a friend come to set free the immortal soul. Death is man's enemy, his ultimate enemy. But God in Christ has shown his authority over death. In the resurrection of Christ he conquered death; in the future resurrection of Christians he will completely destroy death (1 Cor. 15:20-26).

2. *Immortality is purely otherworldly; resurrection is tied in with the person's life in the body.* Those who believe in immortality are sometimes indifferent about physical life in the body: The immortal soul is what counts, not the mortal body. Cultivating the soul and spiritual things is important; what a person does with his body or in his bodily life is unimportant.

At best this view ignores the importance of our bodily existence. At worst some people have assumed that a person whose immortal soul is saved can do as he pleases with his mortal body. This kind of thinking appeared in some forms of gnosticism in the early Christian era. Paul was opposing such twisted thinking in 1 Corinthians 6:12-20. Some Corinthians were justifying sexual immorality by saying that sex is only a function of a mortal body, therefore not a real moral issue. Paul's reply repeatedly stressed the idea of the "body" as the person himself. A person is inseparable from his body. His physical body is mortal, but he himself (the body of his total personality) will share in the resurrection. Therefore, the body is God's temple, and a Christian is to glorify God in his body.

The point is that the resurrection body will be a continuation of life in the physical body. The bodies are not of the same substance, but both are forms of the same human personality. This means that the attitudes and actions, the decisions and the habits of earthly life are inescapably linked to what we will be in eternity. The person I am becoming is the person I will be.

3. *Immortality focuses on the survival of an individual after death; resurrection focuses on the fulfillment of God's hope for all his people.* The idea of the immortality of the soul is concerned primarily with *my* survival beyond death. By contrast, resurrection is a corporate, not an individual concept. For example, in Ezekiel 37 the entire nation was raised from the dead. The same is true in the New Testament. Some in Thessalonica were concerned about the Christian dead. Paul reassured them that the resurrection would include all God's people—those dead in Christ and those still alive (1 Thess. 4:13-18). In Romans 8:18-23 Paul taught that the redemption of our bodies will take place concurrently with the redemption not only of God's children but also of God's entire creation. That is, the resurrection relates to the consummation of God's hope or plan for the redemption of man and nature.

Earlier we noted that the Christian hope is the one hope that God's people share with God himself. Individual hopes of surviving death are like all of the other hopes people have; these hopes are empty and *delusive* unless they are part of God's one hope.

When will the resurrection take place? Some Christians believe that since time will no longer matter in eternity, the resurrection takes place at death. This interpretation, however, misses the reason why the New Testament always places the resurrection at the time of Christ's return. Only then can all the redeemed share fully in the fulfillment of God's hope.

Meanwhile, what of the dead in Christ? Are they merely sleeping as they await the resurrection? Although Jesus and Paul at times used "sleep" as an analogy for death, their point was not that the dead are in a state of unconsciousness. Jesus spoke to the dying thief of paradise on that very day (Luke 23:34). And Paul expressed his own hope of departing and being with Christ (Phil. 1:23).

Thus the New Testament presents these two truths: (1) The dead in Christ go immediately to be with the Lord; (2) The final resurrection will occur when Christ returns. To some people these truths seem irreconcilable, but actually they are complementary: When a Christian dies, he goes to be with the Lord. However, even the dead in Christ share in the hope of final redemption. Their hope is not fulfilled because they as individuals have made it to heaven. To the contrary they continue to await the final goal toward which God is moving human history.

Suppose your family has agreed to meet at a certain time and place for a reunion. Suppose you arrive at the scheduled place before the entire family has gathered. You are already there, but the reunion cannot really begin until all the family is there. Likewise, the dead in Christ are already with the Lord. Their fellowship with him is already rich and wonderful. However, even they await the final resurrection when we all will be clothed with the fullness God has prepared for his own.

The Hope of His Coming

"We do not know what is coming, but we know who is coming—Christ." This motto has often been used by Christians to express their hope. The motto is an accurate expression of the goal of Christian hope as set forth in the New Testament. God is moving history toward its fulfillment in the coming of Christ.

Titus 2:11-14 is one of many New Testament passages that describes this hope. This passage is especially important because it brings together the past and the present as well as the future aspects of this hope. Christians are "awaiting our blessed hope, the appearing of the glory of our great God and Savior Jesus Christ" (v. 13). This is the same Christ "who gave himself for us to redeem us from all iniquity" (v. 14). Our present responsibility is "to renounce irreligion and worldly passions, and to live sober, upright, and godly lives in this world" (v. 12).

All three of these aspects of hope are essential for the full New Testament view of hope in Christ's coming. Take, for example, the relation between the future coming of Christ and his incarnate coming. At times some people have detached the future hope from its moorings in the past. When this happens, we tear away the very foundation of our future hope. Our future hope in Christ's coming is grounded in the life, death, and resurrection of Jesus Christ.

Oscar Cullmann in *Christ and Time* compares Christ's incarnate coming to the decisive battle in a war and Christ's final coming to the end of the war. The decisive battle may be fought long before the final day of victory comes, but the decisive battle settles the final outcome. In the same way Christ's death and resurrection declared the final outcome of God's purpose. The struggle between good and evil rages on, but the final triumph of God's good purpose is assured.

Some people detach hope from its moorings in the past; others go to the opposite extreme and lose the brightness of the future hope. Those who see only the past and present aspects of faith and love are robbing the Christian gospel of its hope and promise.

Faith, love, and hope are inseparably bound together. Paul mentioned this triad of Christian virtues several times (1 Thess. 1:3; 5:8; 1 Cor. 13:13; Col. 1:4-5). The sequence is faith, hope, and love in 1 Corinthians 13:13; but the order is usually faith, love, and hope. This does not mean that faith relates only to the past; love, to the present; and hope, to the future. All three relate to past, present, and future. First Corinthians 13:13 seems to make love the greatest of the three. This is doubtlessly true from one point of view; yet Paul could not describe love without faith and hope: He wrote, "Love believes all things, hopes all things" (1 Cor. 13:7). In Colossians 1:4-5 Paul made hope a force in motivating faith and love.

Thus those who lose the biblical vision of future hope are also impoverishing Christian faith and love. Because "hope springs eternal in the human breast," men will seek something to hope for. When robbed of the Christian hope, they will concoct other hopes. This is one reason why Marxism and other secular rivals of Christianity have arisen. Marxism is strongly futuristic; it offers mankind something to hope for. From the Christian viewpoint, what is offered is a bogus hope. However, one reason for its popularity is the vacuum left by the absence of vital Christian faith, love, and hope.

What do Christians mean when they say, "We do not know what is coming, but we do know who is coming—Christ"? From a negative point of view, we are confessing that we are ignorant of the details of the future; from a positive point of view, we are affirming that we believe that the future lies in God's hands. He is moving history toward the fulfillment of his own redemptive plan and hope.

Some people claim to know all the details of the future as

it relates to Christ's coming. They are claiming to know more than any person knows. For example, every so often someone will claim to know the time of Christ's coming—this in spite of Jesus' clear teaching that no man knows this (Mark 13:32).

Far more important than the exact sequence of events in connection with Christ's coming is the meaning of his coming. His coming represents the goal of Christian hope because it includes the realization of our relationship with God, the consummation of our salvation, and the fullness of our relationship with all God's people.

When Christ comes, we will be "with the Lord" (1 Thess. 4:17). By faith we are already with him. When we die, we will be with him in an even closer way. But when he returns, we shall know a rich, eternal fellowship beyond anything we now experience—although our future relationship with him is a direct outgrowth of our present communion with him.

Likewise, when Christ comes, we will be "like him." "See what love the Father has given us, that we should be called children of God; and so we are. . . . Beloved, we are God's children now; it does not yet appear what we shall be, but we know that when he appears we shall be like him, for we shall see him as he is. And every one who thus hopes in him purifies himself as he is pure" (1 John 3:1-3). This is what the New Testament means by "the hope of salvation" (1 Thess. 5:8) and "the hope of righteousness" (Gal. 5:5). We have been saved from sin's penalty; we are being saved from its power; we shall be saved from its presence. When Christ comes, not only will we see him with an undimmed vision but we also will be made like unto him. This process, of course, is already at work because anyone who has such a hope already is seeking to purify himself as Christ is pure.

When Christ comes, we shall be one in him. The one hope of God's calling as described in Ephesians 1:18 and 4:4 will be realized. The family of God will be together in the house of our Father and we shall dwell together as brothers in perfect love. The new humanity that Paul saw only in the vision of hope will become a reality. This vision calls us to be ministers of reconciliation here and now (for more on this, see chapter 5).

God's Pilgrim People

"Christ—the Hope of the World" was the main theme of the Second Assembly of the World Council of Churches which met in Evanston in 1954. Several years prior to the meeting, an Advisory Commission was appointed to prepare a report on the theme. Sharp differences of opinion were expressed in the early meetings of the Commission. Two divergent points of view about how Christian hope would be realized were apparent. One point of view stressed God's work in bringing in his kingdom; the other point of view stressed man's responsibility in seeking to serve God in the here and now.

The former point of view was voiced primarily by Europeans who had just emerged from the devastation of World War II. They had been in situations of extreme need from which it seemed only God could deliver them. Man's efforts at a brave new world had ended in the horror of the worst war in human history. Thus they had little confidence in man's ability to create a better world.

The latter point of view was expressed primarily by Americans who had been spared the kind of devastation the war brought to Europe. The American representatives, therefore, were not so pessimistic about what men of faith could do to fulfill God's purpose in the world.

Which group was right? There was truth in both points of view. This is the paradox of Christian hope: on one hand, only God can make his hope a reality; on the other hand, God calls us to pray for and work for the coming of his kingdom. Thus there is a sense in which Christian hope means waiting patiently, and there is another sense in which Christian hope means acting diligently.

Waiting and acting are both essential. Perversions of Christian hope appear when either is neglected: Those who stress the waiting without the acting tend to make peace with the status quo. They resign themselves to accepting things as they are—even the things that God wants changed. Those who stress the acting without the waiting fall into the opposite snare. If they are not careful, they will soon conclude that man has little need for God in creating a better world. This then becomes little more than a pious kind of humanism.

The book of Hebrews pictures Christians as God's pilgrim people. "Hope" is a dominant word and theme in Hebrews. As believers in Christ, we have a "better hope" (7:19) than those under the old covenant. Because we know Christ, we have hope as "a sure and steadfast anchor of the soul" (6:19). However, even though we are under the new covenant, we—like the people of Israel—are called "to seize the hope set before us" (6:18). Much has been fulfilled, but much remains yet unrealized. Thus we are called forth on a new exodus as God's pilgrim people (11:1,13).

The book of Hebrews seems to have been written to some Jewish Christians who had made peace with the status quo. They were not pressing on in the world mission to which God had called them. They were remaining safely within the security of "things as they are." Thus, the writer called them to recognize the meaning of Christian hope. Hope always challenges "things as they are" with the vision of things as they can be, should be, and shall be by God's grace. This kind of hope calls at times for patient waiting and at other times for earnest and concerted action.

The concept of Christians as God's pilgrim people is still valid. Christian hope furnishes a vision of God's goal for us and for mankind as a whole. God has called us not just to wait for

him to make the vision a reality. Rather he has called us to
set forth on a pilgrimage toward the goal of Christian hope.
Thus we are on our way, but we are not yet there. Our hope
is not yet sight (Rom. 8:24-25). On one hand, we see in ourselves
and in our world how far God is from the fulfillment of his
hope. Sometimes we are tempted to give up and to resign ourselves to accept things as they are. But the vision of hope summons us to continue on in our pilgrimage. And all along the
way God gives us experiences to remind us of his presence with
us now and of what he is preparing for the future.

Like Christian and Hopeful in John Bunyan's great allegory
The Pilgrim's Progress, we encounter many things that would
halt or hinder our pilgrimage. Many people call us "fools." They
challenge our pilgrimage of hope in the name of realism. In
one sense they are right; hope is "unrealistic" in the sense that
it does not reflect the real world as it is. But hope is not finally
unrealistic because Christian hope challenges us to do something
more than accept and reflect things as they are. Christian hope
calls us to narrow the gap between things as they are and things
as they can be and shall be by God's grace.

Summary

1. Hope is a blessing or a curse depending on whether a person
has made God his hope.

2. Christian hope means sharing God's redemptive hope, not
expecting God to fulfill all our own hopes.

3. Because of the resurrection of Jesus Christ, Christians have
confident hope of life after death.

4. The Christian hope of life after death is not an individual
hope of surviving death (as in immortality of the soul) but a
corporate hope of sharing in the resurrection of all God's people.

5. When Christ comes, Christians will be with him, made like
him, and created one in him.

6. As God's pilgrim people, Christians are called by their

vision of hope to move beyond things as they are toward things as they can be and shall be by God's grace.

---

[1] Ethel Rogers Mulvaney, "The Dawn of Hope," *Guideposts,* April, 1962.

[2] Samuel Beckett, *Waiting for Godot* (New York: Grove Press, 1954), pp. 35,60.

[3] William Owen Carver, *The Glory of God in the Christian Calling* (Nashville: Broadman Press, 1949), p. 104.

[4] Gore Vidal, *The Best Man* (Boston: Little, Brown and Company, 1960), pp. 41-42.

[5] D. P. Brooks, *Dealing with Death—a Christian Perspective* (Nashville: Broadman Press, 1974), p. 59.

joy —celebrating life 4

H. L. Mencken once defined Puritanism as "the haunting fear that someone, somewhere, may be happy." Mencken's definition fits the popular conception of the Puritans as unhappy people who did their best to dampen the happiness of others. This caricature of the Puritans is probably overdrawn, but it is not completely untrue. Judged by modern standards, the Puritans were a rather somber group.

Many people believe that Mencken's definition is true not only of Puritanism but also of Christianity in general. They think of Christ and his followers as killjoys. This misconception is a key factor in keeping many people from becoming followers of Christ; they are convinced that becoming a Christian would put an end to happiness. As evidence of this fact, they point to many professing Christians who seem to lead a drab, joyless existence. Such religion seems only a heavy burden to be borne, not an experience of joy.

What a complete misunderstanding of Christ and his way! Christ is the joy-giver and his way is a way of joy. Christ spoke of his joy and of the full joy he had come to bring to others (John 15:11). "Great joy" was a distinctive characteristic of those who followed him (Acts 8:8; 15:3). Of course, Christ did not come to create a happiness cult. The paradoxical statements of the Beatitudes make this very plain (Matt. 5:3-12). The kind of joy he came to bring is different from what many people think of as happiness. Real joy runs deep and lasts long. Real joy is deeper than laughter and smiles, although laughter and smiles are often expressions of it. Jesus certainly did not teach a dour, long-faced religion. In fact, he warned his followers against such by saying, "Do not look dismal" (Matt. 6:16).

Thus, in spite of the charges of critics and the actions of some professing Christians, Christianity is a way of joy. The word "joy" is found over 150 times in the Bible. (When such words as "joyous" and "joyful" are included, the number comes to about 200.) The verb "rejoice" appears well over 200 times. Both "joy" and "rejoice" occur throughout both the Old Testament and the New Testament. A number of Greek and Hebrew words convey the ideas of joy and rejoicing. We have the same situation in English with such nearly synonymous words as joy, happiness, pleasure, delight, gladness, merriment, felicity, and enjoyment. The words "joy" and "rejoice" are the words used most frequently to translate the Hebrew and Greek words into English. The most characteristic Greek word for "joy" is *chara* (*chairō* is the verb form for "rejoice").

Joy is a little word in both Greek (*ch* is one letter in Greek, so *chara* is a four-letter word) and English. But "joy" is a little word only in size; in concept and scope it is a big word. "Joy" is another one of God's big little words. Joy is a basic human need, and God's intention is that we experience his joy.

Here are some of the questions that we need to try to answer as we probe the meaning and scope of Christian joy: How does joy differ from what many think of as happiness? How does a person get this joy? What is the secret of full joy? What does the Bible mean by "rejoicing in trials"? Why should Christians be able to get more joy out of earthly life than other people do?

Joy Versus Pleasure

"We hold these truths to be self-evident, that all men are created equal, that they are endowed by their Creator with certain unalienable Rights, that among these are Life, Liberty and the pursuit of Happiness." These familiar words are in the Declaration of Independence. Thomas Jefferson, the chief architect of the document, was influenced in many ways by the English philosopher John Locke. Locke, for example, spoke of fundamental human rights which he specified as life, liberty, and property. Jefferson adopted part of this list, but he substituted "happiness" for "property." Thus, our Declaration of Independence affirms as basic God-given human rights "life, liberty, and *the pursuit of happiness.*"

This affirmation is consistent with the teachings of the Bible. God intends for people to have life, liberty, and happiness. However, there are two contrasting theories about human happiness. The Bible commends one of these as the way to real and lasting joy, but it condemns the other as both deceptive and deadly. Generally speaking, the Bible distinguishes between these two theories by using two different words. The word "joy" is the way of true happiness; the word "pleasure" usually refers to the way of false happiness.

The Greek word for "pleasure" is *hēdonē.* This is the word from which comes our English word "hedonism"—the philosophy that pleasure is the chief goal of man. The ways in which this word is used in the New Testament provide guidelines for distinguishing true happiness from false happiness.

Second Timothy 3:4 refers to certain false teachers as "lovers of pleasure rather than lovers of God." This is a basic difference. Joy is a fruit of a right relationship to God. By contrast, pleasure-seeking is a way of life apart from God and contrary to God's will. Pleasure itself is enthroned as a kind of deity to be sought and worshiped.

The word "pleasure" is used in James 4:1 and 3 to characterize a way of life that is filled with selfishness and strife. (Some translations have "lusts" or "passions" here, but it is the same word *hēdonē.*) The selfish desire for one's own happiness or pleasure is the root of much of the quarreling and fighting in the world. (The word "pleasure" in our English Bible is not always a translation of *hēdonē,* nor is "pleasure" always used in a bad sense. See, for example, Phil. 2:13.)

Basically this self-centered view of human happiness assumes that every person has a right to try to grab whatever happiness he wants and to do it however he can. The will of God and the needs of others are ignored by those who follow this way to its logical and deadly conclusion.

This is the way pleasure-seekers interpret "the pursuit of happiness" in the Declaration of Independence. The pleasure-seeker believes he is free to pursue his own happiness no matter what the cost. For example, how many callous, selfish acts are rationalized by saying: "Everyone has his right to happiness; I'm just claiming what is mine."

Joy and fulfillment are part of God's will for each of us, but no one really finds joy or fulfillment by ignoring the will of God and the needs of others. This is not to deny that pleasure offers some thrills and satisfactions. However, pleasure is condemned in the Bible precisely because it cuts off a person from the real joys of life. Instead, it offers a poor imitation. This imitation happiness wears thin over the long haul, and in the end it leaves a person empty.

The Bible makes this very clear. The writer of Ecclesiastes, for example, tried to find satisfaction in various ways. At one stage in his experience he tried pleasure, but his testimony is that this left him empty and disillusioned (2:1-11). His experience has been duplicated repeatedly throughout human history. This kind of experience is epitomized in the words of Proverbs 14:13: "Even in laughter the heart is sad."

Lord Byron in this passage from *Childe Harold* expressed the frantic yet hopeful search for pleasure:

> On with the dance! let joy be unconfined;
> No sleep till morn, when Youth and Pleasure meet
> To chase the glowing Hours with flying feet.

Many believe that *Childe Harold* expressed Lord Byron's own pilgrimage in search for happiness. His last poem was entitled "On This Day I Complete My Thirty-sixth Year." This melancholy passage is clearly autobiographic:

> My days are in the yellow leaf;
>   The flowers and fruits of love are gone;
> The worm, the canker, and the grief
>   Are mine alone!

Robert Burns in "Tam O'Shanter" used four graphic analogies to describe the transient nature of pleasure:

> But pleasures are like poppies spread:
> You seize the flow'r, its bloom is shed;
> Or like the snow falls in the river,
> A moment white—then melts for ever;
> Or like the borealis race,
> That flit ere you can point their place;
> Or like the rainbow's lovely form
> Evanishing amid the storm.

The New Testament warns that self-indulgent pleasure-seeking robs people of the possibility of fruitful living (Luke 8:14). Further it enslaves people in a kind of vicious cycle of addiction (Titus 3:3). The self-indulgent person, according to 1 Timothy 5:6, is dead while she (or he) seems still to live.

Many thoughtful observers have noted that our American preoccupation with fun and excitement is actually evidence of how sad and miserable many people are. Elton Trueblood, for example, has said, "What a sad people it must be that put this much emphasis on fun!" [1] In other words, the frantic attempt to have a good time is often a form of escapism. But the medicine never cures the real disease of our unhappiness. At best, it provides only a temporary respite and in the end we are worse off than before.

Probably the greatest indictment against pleasure-seeking is that it robs a person of the very thing he is seeking most frantically—happiness. Those who get on the treadmill of pleasure-seeking miss the real joys of life that are the gifts of God to all of us who will accept them. As we shall see later, the biblical definition of joy is by no means confined to what some people would call strictly "religious" experiences; the Bible's definition of joy is as broad as God's goodness, which encompasses all of life.

Several years ago a minister attended one of the traditional Army-Navy football classics in Philadelphia. It was one of the most thrilling games he had ever seen. Every known thrill in football was a part of that game. From the opening kickoff until the final gun it was an exciting experience. Navy scored in the last few seconds and the game ended at 20-20.

The minister was sitting behind a man who had brought his excitement in a different form—in a bottle. By the end of the first half the man was drunk. By the end of the third quarter he was asleep. By the end of the game he had slumped to the stadium floor in a drunken stupor.

The drunken man was a tragic figure for many reasons. Part of the tragedy was that he missed the thrills, excitement, the sheer joy and pleasure of the game. In a sense this is a parable on the difference between real and counterfeit happiness. Counterfeit happiness promises but does not deliver real happiness. The pleasure it affords is temporary at best, and in the process of grasping that pleasure a person misses the joy that God has built into life for those who will accept God's joy.

God's Joy and Ours

A small girl was taking her first train ride. When night came,

her parents put her to bed in an upper berth. Although they
assured her that their berths were nearby, the child was a little
uneasy. Therefore, she called out, "Daddy, are you there?" Then
after a while, she would call out, "Mama, are you there?" Despite
their reassuring responses, the little girl continued at regular
intervals to ask her questions. This was annoying one tired
traveler. Finally his patience reached a breaking point. The next
time the child asked her question, she heard an irritated, gruff
voice say: "Yes, your daddy is here. Your mama is here. I am
here. We are all here. Now be quiet and go to sleep." There
was a period of silence and then the little girl called out in
a whisper, "Daddy, was that God?"

Many people think of God in this way—as harsh, gruff, impa-
tient. This misconception is as common as the sentimentalized
view of God as the innocuous, indulgent "man upstairs." God
is neither a grumpy old tyrant nor a supernatural Santa Claus.
The Bible speaks of God as the eternal Creator before whom
we stand in awe and reverence. But the eternal Creator is also
the heavenly Father who loves us in spite of our sins. He is
the living God who wants us to know life—abundant and eternal.
He is the God of love who loves us and calls us to a life of
self-giving love. He is the God of hope who fires our souls with
confident hope. And he is the God of joy who calls us to rejoice
with him and in him.

In Job 38:7 the Lord referred to the time of creation "when
the morning stars sang together, and all the sons of God shouted
for joy." Psalm 104:31 speaks of God himself rejoicing in his
creative work. The Old Testament also speaks of God rejoicing
over his redeemed people who will be to him "a joy" (Isa. 65:18).
Isaiah 62:5 says: "As the bridegroom rejoices over the bride,
so shall your God rejoice over you."

Luke 15 is the most familiar biblical reference to God's joy.
The Pharisees and scribes had criticized Jesus for receiving
sinners and eating with them. Then Jesus told three parables—the

lost sheep, the lost coin, and the loving father (usually called the prodigal son). The explicit theme of each parable is the heavenly joy over one sinner who repents. Verse 7 refers to "joy in heaven"; verse 10 refers to "joy before the angels of God." Verse 32 shows that the joy in heaven includes not only the angels but also God himself. The father in the parable received the returning prodigal with joy. When the elder brother (who represents the attitude of the Pharisees) refused to share this joy, the father (who represents God our Father) explained: "It was fitting to make merry and be glad, for this your brother was dead, and is alive; he was lost, and is found."

In earlier chapters, we have seen that *life, love,* and *hope* are first of all qualities of God and then gifts from God. The same is true of joy. God is a God of joy; joy is part of his very nature. Because of this, the God of joy shares the gift of joy with his creatures. In other words, our joy is a gift from God who is joy.

The joy of God came to focus in human history in Jesus Christ. The heart of Luke's familiar account of the birth of Jesus is the announcement of the angel to the shepherds: "Be not afraid; for behold, I bring you good news of a great joy which will come to all the people; for to you is born this day in the city of David a Savior, who is Christ the Lord" (Luke 2:10-11). The word "joy" is at the heart of the good news which is the gospel of Jesus Christ. This note of joy and exultation runs through the entire biblical account of the coming of Christ (Luke 1:14,44; Matt. 2:10).

> Joy to the world! the Lord is come;
> Let earth receive her King;
> Let every heart prepare Him room,
> And heaven and nature sing. [2]

This note of joy in the Gospels is not confined to the announcement of Christ's coming. Jesus was the Suffering Servant, a man of sorrows and acquainted with grief; but he was also the giver of life and joy. Elton Trueblood in his book *The Humor of Christ* has helped us to see that Jesus was not a joyless, morose person but a man who knew both deep sorrow and deep joy. Reference has already been made to the note of joy in the parables in Luke 15. Joy is also the theme of one of his shortest parables: "The kingdom of heaven is like treasure hidden in a field, which a man found and covered up; then in his joy he goes and sells all that he has and buys that field" (Matt. 13:44).

Those who met Jesus and received him found a new joy and release. Zacchaeus, for example, had been bound tightly in a web mostly of his own making. Then one day Zacchaeus met Jesus. Jesus called him by name and asked to visit with him. Then Zacchaeus, who was in a tree, "made haste and came down, and received him joyfully" (Luke 19:6). Zacchaeus, like the man in the parable of Matthew 13:44, had found a treasure of far greater worth than all he possessed. Joyfully he cast all else aside in order to know Jesus.

As the time of his death approached, Jesus told his followers that soon they would sorrow like a woman in labor but that their sorrow would be turned into joy (John 16:20-22). Later they understood what he meant when the dark sorrow of the cross gave way to the joy of the resurrection (Luke 24:14). Viewed from that perspective, eventually they came to see that the cross itself was necessary for the joy to become real (Heb. 12:2).

Luke 24:52 records a remarkable fact. After the Lord's ascension, his followers "returned to Jerusalem with great joy." These followers had been completely dispirited not many days earlier. They had repeatedly objected to Jesus' words about the need for him to go away. Now he was going away and these same disciples were filled with great joy. Their joy, of course, came from his resurrection and from their anticipation of the continued leadership of the Lord's Spirit.

The book of Acts tells how joy continued to characterize those who followed Jesus. For example, after Philip proclaimed the good news in Samaria, the people believed and "there was much joy in that city" (Acts 8:8). After the work of Paul and Barnabas in Antioch of Pisidia "the disciples were filled with joy and with the Holy Spirit" (Acts 13:52). Paul and Barnabas reported such conversions to other believers, "and they gave great joy to all the brethren" (Acts 15:3). After the conversion of the Philippian jailer, "he rejoiced with all his household that he had believed in God" (Acts 16:34).

People experience joy in different ways, but true joy is a result of a personal encounter with Jesus Christ. Not everyone has a clear-cut, deeply emotional conversion experience, but some do. Blaise Pascal's account of his own joy in Christ is among the most remarkable records of this kind of experience. The record is all the more remarkable because Pascal was a genius whose varied talents made him one of the greatest men of the seventeenth century. He was a mathematician, a physicist, and a philosopher of wide renown. He also became a Christian, a theologian, a saint. Here is his description of his encounter with Christ. Words obviously fail to do full justice to what happened, but notice how often Pascal used *joy* to try to convey his feelings.

FIRE

God of Abraham, God of Isaac, God of Jacob, not of the
     philosophers and scholars.
Certitude. Certitude. Feeling. Joy. Peace.
God of Jesus Christ
Deum meum et Deum vestrum.
"Thy God shall be my God."
Forgetfulness of the world and everything, except God.
     He is to be found only in the ways taught in the Gospel.
     Greatness of the human soul.
     "Righteous Father, the world hath not known
Thee, but I have known Thee."
     Joy, joy, joy, tears of joy. [3]

The Secret of Full Joy

"I have had more fun than any other man in the world. I have never met anyone who has had such fun as I have had." Who do you think spoke these words? One of the world's playboys who devoted his life to pursuing every possible pleasure? An adventurer who experienced the thrill of daring to do the impossible? An entertainer who knew the excitement of success and fame? "I have had more fun than any other man in the world." These words were spoken by Frank Laubach, whose life was dedicated to service to others. Laubach's missionary work was aimed at cultivating literacy among backward people. Laubach found that he could bring great joy to others in this way. In the process of giving joy, he himself found great joy.

John 15:11 is a key verse. Jesus had taught his followers about abiding in him and in his love. He explained that abiding in his love means doing the Father's will. Then Jesus said: "These things I have spoken to you, that my joy may be in you, and that your joy may be full." Jesus prayed for his followers that they might have his joy fulfilled in them (John 17:13). Jesus obviously intended that we know the full joy that was his in doing the will of his Father.

Moral and spiritual life in England in the early eighteenth century was influenced by a short book with a long, forbidding title, *A Serious Call to a Devout and Holy Life.* When the book appeared in 1728, the author William Law prayed that it might have some effect in revitalizing Christian faith, which was at a low ebb. As a young man, John Wesley read the book and was influenced by it. Samuel Johnson, the literary giant of that century, said that Law's book first aroused him to thinking earnestly about religion.

Unfortunately Law's book is seldom read today. The title itself would be enough to frighten away most modern readers. A more appropriate title might be "The Secret of Full Joy." Most religion in 1728 was a boring, dry-as-dust kind of thing. Joy was completely absent. William Law's thesis was that Christ intends for us to have full joy. Further, Law declared that the degree to which we are committed to Christ and his will determines the degree of our joy. Contrary to popular opinion, then and now, real joy is in direct proportion to the degree of genuine Christianity a person has experienced.

Most people simply do not believe this. As evidence, they point to the joyless existence of many religious people. Many Christians look at their own rather dull religious experience and wonder why there is so little joy. Some of these people once knew real joy in Christ; now they wonder what happened: "Where did the glow go?"

The answer is that the Christian life is based on a personal relationship with God. Such a relationship—like all personal relationships—calls for nurture, renewal, communion, commitment. When something disrupts our relationship with God, joy is diminished. David's words in Psalm 51 bear sad testimony to what can happen when sin disrupts a believer's fellowship with God. "Restore to me the joy of thy salvation" (v. 12). "Fill me with joy and gladness" (v. 8). These words were part of David's earnest plea. There is no misery like that of a believer who has lost the joyful awareness of God's presence because of sin. The good news of Psalm 51 and of the Gospels is that God will forgive and restore—his joy can be known again!

David may not be the best example to use because we too often feel a little self-righteous when we think of David's sins of adultery and murder. By comparison the sins of most of us seem harmless and rather tame. The problem for many Christians is not the greatness of our sins but the smallness of our commitment. Many people have just enough religion to make them miserable. Peter Marshall hit the nail on the head: "We are too Christian really to enjoy sinning and too fond of sinning really to enjoy Christianity." [4] What a sorry state of affairs! We have just enough religion to make us unable really to enjoy the pleasures of sin. Our guilty consciences raise too many objections. On the other hand, we have never really gotten serious about Christ and his way. This halfhearted status robs us of the joy that could be ours if we were completely committed to Christ and his will for us.

The paradox of full joy is that no one finds it by seeking it. The one least likely to find full joy is the person who makes this his chief goal. Joy is not a goal for a Christian; it is a fruit of fulfilling the true goals of discipleship—faith in God, obedience to his will, loving service to others. A young couple felt a call to serve as foreign missionaries. When they told their parents, the would-be missionaries encountered opposition. The natural instincts of both sets of parents were against seeing their children head out on such a mission far from home and country. But the longer they talked the more aware the parents became of the determination of the young people. Finally, grudgingly, the parents said: "Well, we see your minds are made up. So if this will make you happy, we won't stand in your way."

The young couple thanked their parents, and then they tried to explain: "You said that we were doing this to make us happy, but this is not why we're doing it. We are doing it because we believe that this is the will of God for us. In many ways this will make us unhappy—leaving behind you and others we love. But although we are not going in order to be happy, we believe that as we do God's will we shall find a deep joy and satisfaction."

Joy in Troubles

"Count it all joy, my brethren, when you meet various trials" (Jas. 1:2). This statement clearly sets forth the aspect of Christian joy that is most difficult to understand and even more difficult to practice. This teaching that Christians can rejoice in trouble is not unique to James. Peter and Paul also mentioned joy and trouble together (1 Pet. 1:6-8; Rom. 5:3-4). And the apostles were but echoing the Master's teaching: Jesus taught his followers to "rejoice and be glad" even when they were persecuted (Matt. 5:12).

Obviously this aspect of Christian joy sets it apart from what people usually define as happiness. By the usual definition, happiness is something that we can seek and sometimes find—if and when the circumstances are such as to produce pleasure and to avoid pain. The Christian view says that joy is not a human achievement. It is a divine gift—a by-product of commitment to God and his will. Because this joy is dependent of doing God's will, it is independent of outward circumstances. Thus a Christian who is doing God's will can rejoice even amid difficult times.

Several factors can help us as we try to understand this paradoxical nature of Christian joy:

1. *Sorrow, pain, and trouble are temporary; joy in the Lord here and now is only a foretaste of the eternal joy we shall know.*— During most of the Old Testament period there was little understanding of life beyond death. Thus believers in times of trouble looked for divine deliverance that would turn sorrow into joy. Psalm 30:5 says, "Weeping may tarry for the night,/ but joy comes with the morning." Some believers, however, made the leap of faith involved in accepting the idea of eternal life. Then they could rejoice not only in the Lord's presence in this life but also in the Lord's continuing presence beyond death. Psalm 16:11 says: "Thou dost show me the path of life;/ in thy presence there is fulness of joy,/ in thy right hand are pleasures for evermore."

This concept of eternal hope and joy is even clearer in the New Testament. Christians can rejoice amid earth's trials because they know that the trials are temporary but the living hope is eternal (1 Pet. 1:3-8; see also Matt. 5:12).

2. *Even when worse comes to worse, we have in God our source of true joy.*—Habakkuk 3:18-19 marks a high point in Old Tes-

tament faith. Many Old Testament believers based their faith squarely on an expectation of long life, success, and good health. God had told Habakkuk that an enemy nation was going to defeat and devastate Judah. The prophet struggled with this, but finally he accepted it; he came to realize that his real life and joy were in the Lord. Therefore, he sang (vv. 17-18):

> Though the fig tree do not blossom,
>   nor fruit be on the vines,
> the produce of the olive fail
>   and the fields yield no food,
> the flock be cut off from the fold
>   and there be no herd in the stalls,
> yet I will rejoice in the Lord,
>   I will joy in the God of my salvation.

Something of the same spirit moved the early Christians to rejoice even when they were mistreated (Acts 5:41). Paul and Silas even sang praises to God amid the dangers and discomforts of the jail in Philippi (Acts 16:25). Later when Paul wrote to the Philippians from a Roman imprisonment, he wrote what has come to be called the "joy epistle." His theme was "Rejoice in the Lord always; again I will say, Rejoice" (Phil. 4:4).

3. *God somehow uses trouble to move us toward what we need to become.*—The full quotation in James reads: "Count it all joy, my brethren, when you meet various trials, for you know that the testing of your faith produces steadfastness. And let steadfastness have its full effect, that you may be perfect and complete, lacking in nothing" (1:2-4). Paul made the same point in Romans 5:3-4: "We rejoice in our sufferings, knowing that suffering produces endurance, and endurance produces character, and character produces hope."

Understanding this principle is not as difficult as practicing it. Winston Churchill took his postwar political defeat very badly. Someone told him to cheer up, for his loss might be "a blessing in disguise," Sir Winston grumpily replied, "If it is, it is surely very well disguised."

C. S. Lewis wrestled intellectually with the theological problem of pain. In his book *The Problem of Pain* he gives the correct answers—insofar as there are any answers. That is, the believer dares to trust in the goodness of God in spite of his pain. He dares to believe that God has some wise and good purpose in allowing his suffering. A painless, troublefree existence is not God's ultimate will for us. His ultimate goal is maturity of faith and life, and sometimes trouble refines faith and develops qualities of character.

Later in his life, Lewis' orthodox principle was tested in the crucible of personal anguish. His beloved wife was dying of cancer, and he was helplessly watching and sharing her torment. Lewis recorded his feelings of doubt and dismay in a series of notebooks. Later he published these in a remarkable little book *A Grief Observed.* The book reads like the biblical book of Job. Like Job, Lewis asked some hard questions of God— questions he left in his book even after he had, to some degree, worked his way through his grief. Also like Job, Lewis never found a satisfying intellectual answer to the specific *why* of his wife's suffering and death. In the depth of his grief at her suffering, he did not doubt God's existence but he doubted God's goodness. God seemed like some kindly surgeon who goes on with his painful surgery because he believes the surgery is necessary in the long run. Eventually Lewis began to make his peace with God by daring to reaffirm his trust that somehow beyond his understanding there is an answer known only to God:

> Heaven will solve our problems, but not, I think, by showing us subtle reconciliations between all our apparently contradictory notions. The notions will all be knocked from under our feet. We shall see that there never was any problem.
>
> . . . .
> And, more than once, that impression which I can't describe except by saying that it's like the sound of a chuckle in the

darkness. The sense that some shattering and disarming simplicity is the real answer. [5]

What about joy? Lewis recalled the joys of their life together prior to her illness. He even testified to the happiness they shared at times during her last days, including her last night. And when she was dying, Lewis writes: "She said not to me but to the chaplain, 'I am at peace with God.' She smiled, but not at me." [6]

Earthly Joys and Eternal Joys

These distinctive qualities of Christian joy are what make joy so preferable to self-indulgent pleasure-seeking. The thesis of the closing section of this chapter is this: The Christian can best enjoy all God's earthly gifts precisely because they are gifts of the God of eternal joy.

Too many people have assumed that God does not want his people to enjoy life. The exact opposite is true. God has called us to joy. The people of faith in Old Testament times celebrated life as God's gift. They made little distinction between what many today would call the "sacred" and the "secular" areas of life. They celebrated the harvest with a feast expressing their joy and gratitude to God (Deut. 16:13-15). They worshiped God with a joyful abandon. Psalm 95:1-2 says:

> O come, let us sing to the Lord;
>   let us make a joyful noise to the rock of our salvation!
> Let us come into his presence with thanksgiving;
>   let us make a joyful noise to him with songs of praise!

The Old Testament calls us to enjoy the goodness of God in the blessings of daily life. Proverbs 5:18 says, "Rejoice in the wife of your youth." The writer of Ecclesiastes, who had found no satisfaction in self-indulgence, commended the enjoyment of honest work and good food (Eccl. 2:24-26). He emphasized that these joys are gifts of God to man.

These teachings are not repealed in the New Testament. First

Thessalonians 5:16 says, "Rejoice always." One of the heresies that confronted the early believers was a form of false spirituality (later called gnosticism) that labeled every earthly thing as evil. First Timothy 4:3 warns against false teachers "who forbid marriage and enjoin abstinence from foods which God created to be received with thanksgiving by those who believe and know the truth." Verses 4-5 explain the biblical view: "For everything created by God is good, and nothing is to be rejected if it is received with thanksgiving; for then it is consecrated by the word of God and prayer."

The New Testament also emphasizes the joy of human relationships. More than once Paul referred to fellow Christians as a joy (1 Thess. 2:19-20; Phil. 4:1). He also instructed believers to share together in the joys and sorrows of life: "Rejoice with those who rejoice, weep with those who weep" (Rom. 12:15). An old English proverb echoes this sentiment: "A sorrow that's shared is but half a trouble. A joy that's shared is a joy made double."

We need to see clearly the distinctions between these kinds of earthly joys and the pleasures of the hedonist:

1. *The basic difference is in a different attitude toward God.*— The Christian rejoices in God above all things. Because of this, he also rejoices in all the good gifts from the God of joy. The Christian does not go out looking for happiness; rather happiness finds him. He seeks not happiness but the glory of God and the good of others. To his surprise, he discovers that joy is his.

This is what C. S. Lewis meant when he entitled his spiritual autobiography *Surprised by Joy.* He had long sought joy (as he understood it); then when God found him and he yielded to God, Lewis was surprised to find the joy he had so long sought.

2. *The Christian rejoices in the gifts of God; he does not seek to manufacture illicit thrills and forbidden pleasures.*—For example, Proverbs 5:15-23 says that a man should rejoice in the wife

of his youth. In this context sex is one of God's good gifts. But self-indulgent sex that regards neither God's laws nor human trusts is a deadly snare. The biblical guidelines about sex are designed to further human joy and fulfillment.

3. *Enjoyment stresses quality, not quantity.*—The pleasure-seeker is basically discontented; he is forever seeking but never finding. He tastes many things, but enjoys few. By contrast, a believer finds greater joy in fewer things. Gratitude and content-ment are part of such joy. Samuel Miller astutely observes:

> It is a strange and ironic fact that in America, where it is so often assumed that we are a thing-loving people, we do not really love things. We make a lot of them; life is cluttered with them; we misuse them, squander them, and waste them; but we do not love them. If we loved them, we would have fewer of them; and in the few we loved, we would see the shadow of that moving grace and power that comes only from God. [7]

In other words we need to discover the wonder that God has built into the daily experiences of life:

Beauty of a sunset
Fragrance of a rose
Warmth of a smile
Taste of good food
Luxury of a night's rest
Fun of being with friends
Thrill of being in love
Exultation of singing
Refreshment of a cool breeze
Excitement of play
Laughter at a joke
Satisfaction of a job well done
Sheer pleasure of being alive
Assurance of God's love and care
Exhilaration of worship
Joy of helping someone

Far too often we rush through life without taking time to enjoy what God has given us. This is a form of ingratitude. This life—this day—this moment is a gift of the God of joy who calls us to know and share his joy.

4. *Earthly joys are foretastes of eternal joys.*—Joy in the Bible always has an eternal dimension to it. Jesus spoke of the rewards of those who are faithful in this life as entering into "the joy" of their Lord (Matt. 25:21,23). Paul often spoke of joy in connection with hope. We are to rejoice in hope (Rom. 5:2; 12:12). He prayed, "May the God of hope fill you with all joy and peace in believing" (Rom. 15:13). This emphasis on the eternal aspect of joy has led some people falsely to assume that Christians should shun earthly joys and fix their eyes on eternal joys. This misses the point. The "eternal" in the Bible is always tied to the earthly; it is the fulfillment, consummation, and perfection of what begins here and now. Thus, earthly joys foreshadow the joys of eternity. They both are gifts from God.

I began this chapter by quoting H. L. Mencken's put-down of Puritanism. G. K. Chesterton, that doughty defender of Christianity, had the temerity to write that the Puritans knew more of real joy than do many pleasure-seekers. He referred specifically to the melancholy hedonism of Omar Khayyam as translated by Edward Fitzgerald. As one reads Fitzgerald's version of the *Rubaiyat,* he cannot escape the haunting shadow of death that hangs over every pleasurable moment. Chesterton wrote that this philosophy of "eat, drink, and be merry, for tomorrow we die" is not a joyful, but a melancholy way of life. He suspected that the dour Puritans, with their faith in God and heaven, stumbled into more sheer joy than the followers of Epicurus and Fitzgerald are able to grasp in spite of all their earnest efforts.

Chesterton sets forth his own view of joy in these words:

> It is true enough, of course, that a pungent happiness comes in certain passing moments; but it is not true that we should

> think of them as passing, or enjoy them simply "for those mo-
> ments' sake." . . . These moments are filled with eternity; these
> moments are joyful because they do not seem momentary. . . .
> Man cannot love mortal things. He can only love immortal things
> for an instant. [8]

Summary

1. The selfish pursuit of pleasure has its thrills, but it destroys the possibility of real and lasting joy.

2. True joy is a gift of the God of joy as we respond to God's grace in Christ and experience the Holy Spirit.

3. The fullness of Christian joy is in direct proportion as we are fully committed to the will of God and the needs of others.

4. The nature of Christian joy is such that it is not destroyed by trouble, pain, and sorrow.

5. The Christian can enjoy all of God's earthly gifts because they are foretastes of God's eternal gifts of joy.

---

[1] Elton Trueblood, "Ideas That Shape the American Mind," *Christianity Today,* 6 January 1967, p. 9.

[2] Isaac Watts, "Joy to the World! The Lord Is Come," *Baptist Hymnal* (Nashville: Convention Press, 1956), p. 65.

[3] Blaise Pascal, *Great Shorter Works of Pascal,* translated with an introduction by Emile Cailliet and John C. Blankenagel (Philadelphia: The Westminster Press, 1948), p. 117.

[4] Peter Marshall, *Mr. Jones, Meet the Master* (New York: Fleming H. Revell Company, 1949), p. 145.

[5] C. S. Lewis, *A Grief Observed* (New York: The Seabury Press, 1961), p. 56.

[6] *Ibid.,* p. 60.

[7] Samuel H. Miller, *Man the Believer* (New York: Abingdon Press, 1968), pp. 111-12.

[8] Gilbert K. Chesterton, *Heretics* (Freeport, N.Y.: Books for Libraries Press, 1905, 1970), pp. 108-109.

peace —everyone's dream 5

"Peace is a good so great, that even in this earthly and mortal life there is no word we hear with such pleasure, nothing we desire with such zest, or find to be more thoroughly gratifying." Thus wrote Augustine in his classic work *The City of God.* Who is there that does not find himself in hearty agreement?

Peace was looked on as the ideal state by almost all the civilizations of ancient times. The Greeks and the Romans even made Peace a goddess. Although wars were common, peace was considered the desirable ideal. The Greek poet Hesiod told of a lost age of gold when peace had once been a reality. According to Hesiod, mankind has passed with deteriorating effects through ages of silver and bronze to an age of iron, during which wars and strife now prevail.

Whatever may have been true in the past, the yearning for peace is intense today. The refinement of new weapons of mass destruction has made peace a matter of absolute priority. Peace is on every lip: Statesmen and diplomats struggle to achieve it. The news media constantly speak of it. The average person hopes and prays for it. Peace, it seems, is everyone's dream.

The word "peace" is as frequent in biblical usage as in modern usage. It is another of God's big little words. The Bible writers shared the ageless human yearning for peace, but they also bear witness to a distinctive meaning and approach to peace—one that is intensely practical and up-to-date.

More Than the Absence of War

The Hebrew word *shalom* is the key to the biblical meaning of peace. The English word "peace," like the Latin *pax* from which it comes, is primarily negative in meaning: "Peace" is primarily used to describe the absence of war and strife and the tranquility resulting thereby. The Greek word *eirēnē* was used in a similar way outside the Bible. Thus, for both the Romans and the Greeks *pax* and *eirēnē* meant the absence of war. However, the Hebrew concept of *shalom* was more positive and comprehensive in meaning.

The basic meaning of *shalom* is well-being or wholeness. The Hebrews used it to describe the total well-being of man and society. The Hebrews saw each person as a whole person, not as something that was to be divided into such separate components as body, mind, and spirit. The modern recognition that each person is a psychosomatic whole is no new insight to those schooled in the Hebraic view of man. And the Hebrews saw each person as a vital part of the wholeness of God's people and creation. Thus, peace had to do with the ideal well-being of man in proper harmony with God, his fellow man, and the rest of God's creation.

The word *shalom* and its derivatives are found over 350 times in the Old Testament. When the Old Testament was translated into Greek shortly before the Christian era, the Greek word *eirēnē* was used to translate *shalom*. Many of the early Christians read and quoted the Greek translation of the Old Testament; therefore, when they used *eirēnē,* they generally used it to mean much more than *eirēnē* had meant prior to its association with *shalom*. Thus *shalom* became the key factor in determining the meaning of *eirēnē* in the New Testament and "peace" as Christians understand it.

At times *shalom* was used to describe the opposite of war. For example, God told David that he could not build the Temple because David had shed so much blood and waged so many wars; the Lord said that the building of the Temple would be entrusted instead to Solomon, who would be "a man of peace" (1 Chron. 22:8-9). Likewise, the writer of Ecclesiastes in his description of the contrasting times and seasons referred to "a time for war, and a time for peace" (Eccl. 3:8).

These two examples, however, are not typical of the Old Testament meaning of *shalom*. Generally it means well-being and wholeness, apart from any reference to the issue of war or peace. For example, as Jacob had his initial encounter with God at Bethel, he made this vow: "If God will be with me, and will keep me in this way I go, and will give me bread to eat and clothing to wear, so that I come again to my father's house in peace, then the Lord shall be my God" (Gen. 28:20-21). Jacob was speaking of his total well-being.

Jeremiah 29:7 is a good example of *shalom* as positive concern for the total well-being of a community. In writing to the Jewish exiles in Babylon, Jeremiah declared this as part of God's word for them: "Seek the welfare of the city where I have sent you into exile, and pray to the Lord on its behalf, for in its welfare you will find your welfare." The word "welfare" is the Hebrew *shalom,* which is translated "peace" in the King James Version. "Peace" here referred to the total welfare of the city of Babylon.

Psalm 122 is a song of worship, not a prayer for peace in time of war. It was probably a hymn of praise sung by pilgrims leaving the holy city. As they left, they sang:

> Pray for the peace of Jerusalem!
>   "May they prosper who love you!
> Peace be within your walls,
>   and security within your towers!"
> For my brethren and companions' sake
>   I will say, "Peace be within you!"
> For the sake of the house of the Lord our God,
>   I will seek your good (vv. 6-9).

This prayer may be an intentional play on words, for the name

Jerusalem incorporates a form of *shalom*. The meaning of Jerusalem seems to be people or habitation of *shalom*.

A complete study of all the instances of *shalom* would confirm the view that these last three references are typical. The word is used in close connection with such words as blessing, prosperity, security, salvation, righteousness, and justice.

Shalom was and still is a word used both as a greeting and as a word of parting. David, for example, sent this greeting to Nabal: "Peace be to you, and peace be to your house, and peace be to all that you have" (1 Sam. 25:6). Such a blessing is obviously much richer than a mere hello. It is wishing someone the best in every sense of the word. Often it is intended as a pronouncement of divine blessing. As Hannah left Shiloh, Eli said to her: "Go in peace, and the God of Israel grant your petition which you have made to him" (1 Sam. 1:17). Our English word "good-bye" was originally used in this way as a kind of benediction: "good-bye" was originally "God be with ye."

The Greek *eirēnē* was used in the New Testament as a common greeting (Jas. 2:16). Jesus used it (Mark 5:34; Luke 7:50), and he told his disciples to use this greeting in their missionary work (Luke 10:5-6). Nearly all of the New Testament epistles begin with this word as a greeting from writer to readers.

The early Christians lived in an era called the *Pax Romana,* the peace of Rome. When Augustus became emperor after a series of bloody civil wars, he closed the gates to the temple of Janus as a sign of peace. Many heralded his reign as a return to the mythical age of gold, when peace was supposed to have existed throughout the earth. His successors continued to try to maintain the *Pax Romana,* with varying degrees of success. From the Roman point of view those centuries were centuries of peace.

It is true that one government ruled the civilized world with some semblance of law and order. But the *Pax Romana* was secured and maintained by bloodshed and warfare. Intermittent civil wars and rebellions continued to plague parts of the Roman Empire. The Jews were among those who rebelled during that period, and the rebellion was put down with typical Roman thoroughness and brutality. Ironically the city of Jerusalem, the city of peace, and the Temple were destroyed during the *Pax Romana*. From the Christian point of view those also were the centuries when the government alternately protected and persecuted believers in Jesus Christ.

Not everyone was enthusiastic about the *Pax Romana*. Many of the conquered people who lived under Roman rule were bitter and cynical. One of the Britons expressed well this point of view: "The Romans are robbers of the world. After denuding the land, they rifle the sea. They are rapacious toward the rich and domineering toward the poor, satiated neither by the East nor by the West. Pillage, massacre, and plunder they grace with the name of empire and where they make a desert, call it peace."

The philosopher Epictetus lived in the last part of the first century and the first part of the second century. He was not completely unaware of the benefits of the *Pax Romana,* but he pinpointed some of its chief limitations: "While the emperor may give peace from war on land and sea, he is unable to give peace from passion, grief, and envy. He cannot give peace of heart, for which man yearns more than even for outward peace."

This brief sketch of the *Pax Romana* reinforces the biblical emphasis on peace as something more than the absence of war. A recent book by Jack Stotts sets forth *shalom* as the most appropriate biblical symbol for Christians in today's world. He writes:

> *Shalom* as a positive, affirmative vision of the well-being and well-doing of the creation transcends any definition of peace that would equate it with the 'cessation of hostilities.' While the end of armed conflict between nations and peoples is ingredient to the *shalom* of God and therefore a condition of life to be vigorously and persistently sought, the peaceable city compre-

hends a quality of life that refuses to be defined negatively as the absence of armed strife. [1]

The God of Peace

During the early days of space exploration the Russian cosmonaut Titov made one of the first successful journeys into space. One of the stories circulated at the time told how Russian Premier Khrushchev privately asked Titov whether he had seen anyone while out in space. According to the story, Titov told Khrushchev that he had seen God. The premier responded, "I knew that already, but you know our policy, so please don't tell anybody."

Later Titov was interviewed by the leading official of the Russian Orthodox Church. The patriarch asked Titov if he had seen God out there. Faithful to his instructions, Titov denied that he had seen God. The church official replied, "I knew that already, but you know our policy, so please don't tell anybody." [2]

This apocryphal story says something about the strange mixture of faith and unbelief in the modern world. Communism is officially atheistic. It is only one form of humanism, the religion of modern, secular man. Humanism denies man's need for God or anything supernatural. According to humanism, modern man can neither believe in God nor does he need to believe in God. Yet the story about Khrushchev suggests that even professed atheists have their doubts about a system that rules out anything beyond man himself. The other part of the story—the part about the patriarch—illustrates the other side of the coin: Those who profess to believe in God are strongly influenced by the humanistic, secular society in which they live. Even those who speak the loudest about their faith are sometimes not so sure.

Thus modern man is a strange mixture of faith and unbelief. On one hand, he is a child of a humanistic society, which assumes that God is an unbelievable and unnecessary hypothesis. On the other hand, many of us are also children of a heritage of faith preserved within Christian teachings.

The question of faith in God is crucial. In each of the preceding chapters we have noted that the Bible considers God the source and giver of life, love, hope, and joy. The same biblical presupposition holds with regard to peace: God is the God of peace—the source and giver of peace.

By contrast, humanism is no less interested in life, love, hope, joy, and peace. These are universal human concerns. The humanist, however, has a completely different presupposition about the source of these coveted experiences: Man apart from any supernatural God must seek to find these qualities for himself. Some humanists are pessimistic about man's ability to attain these goals; other humanists are optimistic. All humanists, however, agree (except in rare moments when they doubt their doubts) that God has nothing to do with the process.

The Bible is equally clear in stating the opposite view: only in God will man find life, love, hope, joy, and peace. The Old Testament refers to God as the source and giver of peace. He speaks peace to his people (Ps. 85:8). The divine blessing of Numbers 6:24-26 expresses this in a memorable way:

> The Lord bless you and keep you:
> The Lord make his face to shine upon you,
>   and be gracious to you:
> The Lord lift up his countenance upon you,
>   and give you peace.

The New Testament repeatedly refers to the "God of peace." Most of these references come near the end of letters. They are either a part of a final benediction or an expression of a divine blessing.

For example, 1 Thessalonians 5:23 reads: "May the God of peace himself sanctify you wholly; and may your spirit and soul and body be kept sound and blameless at the coming of our Lord Jesus Christ." (See also Rom. 16:20; 2 Cor. 13:11; Phil. 4:9; and Heb. 13:20.)

Among the most intriguing biblical references to "peace" are those in which some of the prophets warned against the superficial peace offered by false prophets. *Shalom* had apparently become a key word for all the prophets, but a bitter debate raged about the nature and source of *shalom.* One group, apparently comprised of official and court prophets, promised peace for the king and the nation. The other group of prophets insisted that there could be no peace so long as the king and people ignored God and his will for them. Micah, Jeremiah, and Ezekiel were the chief representatives of the latter group. Jeremiah, for example, spoke these words for God (6:13-14):

> For from the least to the greatest of them,
>   every one is greedy for unjust gain;
> and from prophet to priest,
>   every one deals falsely.
> They have healed the wound of my people lightly,
>   saying, "Peace, peace,"
> when there is no peace.

These biblical prophets accused the people not of actual atheism but of practical atheism; that is, the people claimed to believe in God, but they denied him by their disregard of God's conditions for peace—justice and human concern (Mic. 3:5-9). The lies of the false prophets condemned the prophets and those who believed them to sure judgment (Ezek. 13:8-16).

The biblical prophets promised that God would offer his repentant people a covenant of peace (Ezek. 37:26). The covenant of peace would be based on God's steadfast love and mercy (Isa. 54:10). Isaiah 57:19-21 promises peace to the penitent but warns persistent sinners of continuing unrest:

> Peace, peace, to the far and to the near, says the Lord;
>   and I will heal him.
> But the wicked are like the tossing sea;
>   for it cannot rest,
>   and its waters toss up mire and dirt.
> There is no peace, says my God, for the wicked.

When the prophets spoke of *shalom,* their words revealed a tension between the actual and the ideal—the present reality and the hoped-for future. On one hand, the prophets had a vision of a future age of peace—when God would reign and men would live in peace. Among the most famous of these passages is Isaiah 2:1-4. The word *shalom* is not found in this passage, but the word does occur in the larger context. Isaiah 9:6 gives this prophecy of the coming of the ideal messianic King:

> For to us a child is born,
>   to us a son is given;
> and the government will be upon his shoulder,
>   and his name will be called
> "Wonderful Counselor, Mighty God,
> Everlasting Father, Prince of Peace."

Zechariah 9:9-10 is another prophetic description of the future King who would bring peace to the nations.

The prophetic visions of a future age of peace were not detached from the prophets' present, practical concern for peace. They called for people of faith to practice all the qualities that make for peace, not just to await a future age of peace. But whether speaking of the present or the future, the prophets always thought of peace as emanating from God, the source and giver of peace.

The Hebrews could work for and hope for peace precisely because they believed that God is in control of history. God is moving history toward a goal, and one comprehensive symbol of that goal is *shalom.* Many people see no divine purpose in human history. Some people think that history merely repeats itself in an endless cycle of human blunders, of which war is the worst. Others deny any divine presence or purpose in history, but they still try to remain optimistic about man's ability to evolve into a society where peace will prevail. From a biblical point of view such a humanistic utopia, even if it were possible, would lack the most distinctive qualities of *shalom*. The key to *shalom* is that fullness of life which comes to us from God—whom to know is life, love, hope, joy, and peace.

Peace with God

The prophetic insights and promises about peace are echoed and amplified in the New Testament: Man's sin against God makes peace impossible, because sin alienates man from the God of peace. God offers sinful man a covenant of peace based on his steadfast love and mercy. The New Testament points to Jesus Christ as the Prince of peace. His mission was to remove sin as a barrier between man and God, to reconcile sinful man to the God of grace, and thus to bring believers into a new state of peace with God. This means that the God of peace calls us to peace with himself through Jesus Christ.

Luke 2:14 is probably the most widely known Bible statement about peace. The song of the heavenly host to the shepherds was: "Glory to God in the highest, and on earth peace among men with whom he is pleased." This translation is more accurate than "peace, good will to men." The key words in the promise are *glory* and *peace*. The coming of Christ means glory to God, and it means peace to men. The words "with whom he is pleased" do not mean that God arbitrarily favors some people and withholds his favor from others. The context of the entire gospel story shows that an accurate paraphrase would be "peace to men, who are the objects of God's grace." In other words, the God of grace offers men peace through Jesus Christ.

Many who met Jesus of Nazareth found this peace. When Jesus spoke the words "go in peace" to one who had come to him in faith, his words had more than the usual significance of a Jewish farewell. For example, these were his parting words to the sinful woman of Luke 7:36-50: "Your faith has saved you; go in peace" (v. 50).

When Jesus entered Jerusalem for the last time, Matthew

clearly cites the royal entry as fulfilling the promise of Zechariah 9:9-10. Jesus was the humble King who came to bring peace. Luke 19:38 records what his followers sang on that occasion: "Blessed is the King who comes in the name of the Lord! Peace in heaven and glory in the highest!" Jesus himself, however, wept as he neared the city, saying, "Would that even today you knew the things that make for peace!" (Luke 19:42.)

His death seemed an utter defeat to his followers at the time. However, his resurrection turned defeat into victory. John's Gospel records how the risen Lord's first words to his assembled followers were " 'Peace be with you' " (20:19; see also vv. 21,26). The disciples reappraised the crucifixion in the light of the resurrection and later in the light of Pentecost. As they did, they saw how Jesus fulfilled the mission of the Suffering Servant of Isaiah 53 (see Acts 8:30-35; 1 Pet. 2:24). The King James Version of Isaiah 53:5 reads, "He was wounded for our transgressions, he was bruised for our iniquities: the chastisement of our peace was upon him; and with his stripes we are healed." The Revised Standard Version renders "the chastisement of our peace" as "the chastisement that made us whole." In other words, his own suffering was in order that we might have peace.

Paul often used the word "grace" to characterize the good news of Jesus Christ, but he also spoke of "the gospel of peace" (Eph. 6:15). Paul used both words—grace and peace—as a greeting in all his letters. The most common form of the greeting was "Grace to you and peace from God our Father and the Lord Jesus Christ" (Rom. 1:7; 1 Cor. 1:3; 2 Cor. 1:2; Eph. 1:2; Phil. 1:2). The usual Greek greeting was *chaire* ("rejoice"). Paul used the closely related word *charis* ("grace"). Thus his greeting was a Christianized adaptation of a combined Greek-Hebrew greeting. For Paul, this was more than a greeting; it was a testimony to the very heart of the Christian gospel.

Paul often used all five of the big little words that we have considered in this book. He often mentioned one or more of them in the same passage. For example, he all but equated life and peace in Romans 8:6. In Galatians 5:22 he wrote of love, joy, and peace as the first three marks of the fruit of the Spirit. In Romans 15:13 he prayed that the God of hope would fill believers with all joy and peace. Perhaps the most comprehensive passage is Romans 5:1-5, where Paul showed the interrelationships between peace, joy, hope, and love. Verse 1 sets the tone for the whole passage: "Therefore, since we are justified by faith, we have peace with God through our Lord Jesus Christ."

Peace with God means a new relationship with God. The barrier of sin has been removed, the sinner has been reconciled, and new life has begun. Peace with God refers not only to the initial sense of salvation and newness of life but also to the growing experience of assurance and wholeness. Thus Paul wrote of "the peace of God, which passes all understanding" (Phil. 4:7).

Perhaps Paul had in mind the legacy of Jesus recorded in John 14:27: "Peace I leave with you; my peace I give to you; not as the world gives do I give to you. Let not your hearts be troubled, neither let them be afraid." Jesus made it plain that he was not promising a tranquil, untroubled life. He said: "I have said this to you, that in me you may have peace. In the world you have tribulation; but be of good cheer, I have overcome the world" (John 16:33). His peace can be known in the midst of troubles. (Compare this fact with the paradoxical statements about joy in trials in chapter 4.)

This "peace with God" or "peace which passes all understanding" is the Bible's answer to man's yearning for inner peace. Countless books on peace of mind attest to the eager quest for this ideal. The Bible comes at this from a distinctive point of view: peace, like joy, is not something we find or achieve for ourselves; it is something that finds us when we lose ourselves in doing God's will. This may be what Jesus meant when he said that his gift of peace was not the kind of peace the world gives. Inner peace is not an achievement; it is a gift, a gift that comes as a fruit of serving Christ and a gift that can be known in the midst of tension and turmoil.

W. E. Sangster dealt with this subject in an article entitled "Can We Get 'Peace of Mind'?" He told how Edward Fitzgerald, the translator of the *Rubaiyat* of Omar Khayyam, sought peace by changing his circumstances and surroundings:

> He parted from the wife whose presence he found disturbing. He left the city and settled in a small country town. He remoulded his circumstances nearer to the heart's desire—and kept doves (because doves are the birds of peace), but peace passed him by! Peace is not found in circumstances; peace is found only in the heart. [3]

Sangster correctly pointed out that peace of mind is not attained by altering circumstances. He also pointed out that the peace Jesus gives can survive some of life's hardest blows:

> Peace that can be destroyed any morning by a letter, or by the headlines in a newspaper, or by a motorist's mistake, or by a doctor's diagnosis, is too brittle for this rough world. Peace that can begin only when all our problems are solved will not begin on this earth. We have to learn to live with problems in ourselves, in society, and in the wider world. If we cannot have peace in a world of change, unsolved problems, and possible disaster, we cannot have it at all. [4]

On Moving Fences

Too much so-called "peace of mind" is only a form of escapism; too many people want inner peace for themselves, but they have no concern for the needs of others. To interpret the Christian's inner peace in this way would be completely to miss the point of Jesus' gift of peace. The peace that Jesus gives is not attained by arranging circumstances to suit ourselves; neither is inner peace found by retreating from involvement in trying to solve the problems of the modern world. Inner peace is never a self-centered enterprise; it always comes in context with seeking the conditions that make for peace in human society. The Bible's words about inner peace are always spoken in the context of God's concern for the well-being and wholeness of others.

During World War II, three American airmen who had escaped from a POW camp made their way to a French village. The French hid them and helped them. While there, one of the escaped prisoners died from sickness and exhaustion. The other two Americans asked the local priest if they could bury their friend in the church cemetery. The priest shook his head and told them, "Only Catholics can be laid to rest in there, but you can bury him in that lot just outside the fence." They buried him there, but during the night the priest and some of the people took down the fence and moved it to include the new grave. The priest explained, "A Protestant may not be buried in the cemetery, but there is no rule that says that we cannot move the fence to include a Protestant." [5]

Our world is a world of fences, walls, and barriers. Many of these reflect the hostility and alienation of various groups in society. The New Testament teaches that God's purpose in Christ is to bring sinners not only to peace with God but also to a new state of peace with one another in Christ.

Paul made this very clear, especially in his letter to the Ephesians. This letter sets forth God's plan or goal for mankind in terms of peace and reconciliation. Paul described how sin had resulted in a two-fold estrangement between God and man and between man and his fellowman. The epitome of the latter alienation was the hostility and prejudice that separated Jews and Gentiles in the first century. Paul described that alienation in Ephesians 2:11-12; then he addressed these words (vv. 13-18) to Gentiles converted to Christianity:

> But now in Christ Jesus you who once were far off have been brought near in the blood of Christ. For he is our peace, who has made us both one, and has broken down the dividing wall

of hostility, by abolishing in his flesh the law of commandments and ordinances, that he might create in himself one new man in place of the two, so making peace, and might reconcile us both to God in one body through the cross, thereby bringing the hostility to an end. And he came and preached peace to you who were far off and peace to those who were near; for through him we both have access in one Spirit to the Father.

This may well be the most important biblical passage on peace. The peace Paul described there represents God's goal, his hope for humanity (see the comments on Eph. 1:18 in chapter 3). The "dividing wall of hostility" referred to an actual wall in the Jewish Temple. The wall separated the Court of the Gentiles from the inner worship area of the Temple. A sign on the wall threatened death to any Gentile who dared to enter. The Gospels record how the veil in the Temple was rent from the top to the bottom when Jesus died (Mark 15:38; Matt. 27:51; Luke 23:45). This veil separated the holy of holies from the rest of the Temple. The tearing of the veil signified the access of man to God through Christ. In Ephesians 2 Paul insisted that the dividing wall which excluded Gentiles also was destroyed by Christ's death. The wall actually stood until A.D. 70 when the Romans destroyed the Temple, but Paul said that, in effect, the death of Christ removed the barrier. Thus, Jews and Gentiles are brought to God and to one another in Christ. The "one new man" mentioned in Ephesians 2:15 is the new humanity that God is seeking to create in Christ. This oneness and wholeness is the peace that Christ came to bring.

Paul never lived to see this ideal hope become a full reality, but he bent his every effort to make this peace an actuality. And he did see many examples of the miraculous working of this peace. He worked and prayed to see each band of believers become a community of love and peace that encompasses all kinds of people. His letters are filled with admonitions for each church to be a model of what Christ's peace can mean: A worthy

Christian life includes an eagerness "to maintain the unity of the Spirit in the bond of peace" (Eph. 4:3).

Paul wrote to the Thessalonians, "Be at peace with one another" (1 Thess. 5:13), words that echo Jesus' admonition in Mark 9:50. In Colossians 3:15 the apostle wrote, "Let the peace of Christ rule in your hearts, to which indeed you were called in one body." Paul clearly had more in mind here than individual peace of mind; he spoke of a peace that bound all the Colossian believers together in one body in Christ.

The real test of such peace comes when tense situations arise in a church fellowship. The Roman church was encountering some tension because of two groups who disagreed about eating meat. Paul was quick to remind them that "the kingdom of God does not mean food and drink but righteousness and peace and joy in the Holy Spirit" (Rom. 14:17). He admonished them, "Let us then pursue what makes for peace and mutual upbuilding" (Rom. 14:19). The Corinthian church caused Paul much grief because of bitter dissension within the church. Paul closed one of his letters to Corinth with these words: "Finally, brethren, farewell. Mend your ways, heed my appeal, agree with one another, live in peace, and the God of love and peace will be with you" (2 Cor. 13:11).

Christians in their relationships with one another should be models of the peace that is God's intention for redeemed humanity. Where such peace prevails in churches and in Christian homes, a powerful testimony for Christ is given to the world. By contrast, what do we communicate to the outside world when Christians cannot practice peace and love toward one another? No amount of fervent preaching and evangelizing can offset the example of a group of Christian brothers who wrangle with one another.

Keep in mind also that peace means more than the absence of conflict. It refers to the positive wholeness of people rightly related to God and one another. Thus peace means not only mutual forbearance but also active love and concern for one another. In their relations with one another too many Christians fail to practice the things that make for peace. Too many are like one couple who could not seem to move beyond past grudges. They admitted sadly: "We often decide to bury the hatchet, but one of us always remembers where it is buried and digs it up again." Someone has defined a Christian family not as a group of perfect people but as a community of forgiving people. The same is true of the family of faith, the church.

Peace and *agapē* are closely related in Christian living. In chapter 2 the qualities and scope of Christian love were set forth. The practice of such self-giving love is an essential ingredient for establishing and maintaining peace in human relations.

The Making of Peacemakers

The scope of Christian love begins with brothers but also includes neighbors and even enemies. In the same way the Christian's concern for peace cannot be restricted to relations with brothers in Christ. Paul wrote, "If possible, so far as it depends upon you, live peaceably with all men" (Rom. 12:18). The context of this statement (vv. 14-21) shows that Paul had in mind a Christian's attempt to live at peace with all people, even his enemies. The same principles set forth by Jesus in Matthew 5:38-48 are assumed by Paul in this passage: Christians are not to strike back at enemies by returning evil for evil. This is the natural and human way of reacting, but Christians are to reverse the deadly cycle of vengeance, grudge-bearing, and retaliation. Instead of giving back evil for evil, Christians are to give back good for evil.

Christians are not only to strive to live at peace with others; we also are admonished to pray for conditions in human society that enable us to "lead a quiet and peaceable life" (1 Tim. 2:2). This is a New Testament echo of Jeremiah's advice to the Jewish exiles in ancient Babylon: They were advised to pray and work for the peace and welfare of the pagan city of Babylon (Jer. 29:7).

The Beatitude in Matthew 5:9 adds a further dimension to Christian responsibility about peace. Jesus said, " 'Blessed are the peacemakers, for they shall be called sons of God.' " We should interpret this statement in the light of the total scope of biblical teachings about peace: God is the source and giver of peace. He himself is the great Peacemaker. Those who share in the divine ministry of peacemaking are recognized as sons of God.

This raises the sensitive question of the Christian's attitude toward and involvement in the issues of war and peace. Historically there has been no one "Christian" pattern of action. Roland H. Bainton has made a careful historical study of *Christian Attitudes Toward War and Peace.* He identifies three general approaches that some Christians have adopted: pacifism, the just war, and the crusade. Advocates of each position have quoted certain Bible verses to justify their position.

Fortunately, most Christians have moved beyond the view that war is ever a holy crusade of the forces of good against the forces of evil. This was the distorted view that spawned the Crusades of the Middle Ages and the bloody persecutions and religious wars of the post-Reformation era.

In modern times, World War I was the last war when a general crusade spirit prevailed among American Christians. The churches, for the most part, were swept up in the spirit of a "war to end all wars," a war that was supposed to "make the world safe for democracy." The spirit of pacifism was strong between World War I and World War II. After Pearl Harbor, American Christians generally supported the war effort against the Axis powers, but Christian statements about participation in the war lacked the crusade mentality. Most of those who went to war did so reluctantly and repentantly.

A favorite Bible text for crusaders is Matthew 10:34: Jesus

said, "Do not think that I have come to bring peace on earth; I have not come to bring peace but a sword." Sometimes a person can take a verse literally but not seriously. We should always take the Bible seriously, but not always literally. A strictly literal interpretation here would create a hopeless contradiction between this statement of Jesus and countless other things he said. As we have seen, the total context of the Bible and multiplied references show that Jesus did come to bring peace, not a sword. Matthew 10:34 was a shocking statement designed to set forth the tension of discipleship in the strongest possible terms. (Compare Luke 14:26, where Jesus called his followers to hate their family members.) Only a person looking for a proof text would ever read Matthew 10:34 as divine justification for a holy war.

Most Christians have been pacifists at heart, but reluctant participants in war when this seemed absolutely necessary. Other Christians have maintained a position of absolute and complete pacifism. Little is to be gained by these two groups judging one another; much is to be gained by these groups working together for peace. Given the conditions of today's world, no Christian could fail to be for peace. And if we take Jesus seriously, no Christian can fail to seek to be a peacemaker on every level of human interaction.

Our dilemma is that peacemaking is the most demanding of all roles. Those who refuse to accept absolute pacifism can point to the fact that peacemaking sometimes demands more than a passive, relinquishing role. The classic example of passive pacifism was Neville Chamberlain, who tried so hard to avoid World War II by a series of concessions to Hitler. Chamberlain returned to England from Munich announcing that he had achieved "peace with honor." He said, "I believe it is peace for our time." Some historians are convinced that World War II might have been avoided had other nations taken a firm, early stand against Hitler's aggressive policies. As it was, Hitler became convinced that he could take whatever he wanted with no outside interference.

The other side of the coin is that war is always the worst of tragedies. Sherman's statement "war is hell" is true to the extent that nothing other than hell itself is so like hell as war. The prospect of nuclear war has added a new dimension of reality to Sherman's definition.

"But what can *I* do?" each of us may ask. Much more than most of us have done! We are citizens in a representative form of government. We are Christians and members of a church and of a denomination. We can exert our individual and corporate influence on behalf of what makes for peace. Douglas J. Harris made a careful study of the biblical meaning of peace. In his concluding chapter he notes the tension in the Bible between the real and the ideal. He sees this tension as a call for Christians to lend their support toward a "will for peace." Harris writes: "The desire for peace is universal; less so, the will to peace. It seems to me that the Christian is called to lend his influence toward the will to peace: peace among men, peace of man with God, and peace among nations." [6]

Pope John XXIII, in his encyclical *Pacem in Terris,* "Peace on Earth," called on all men of goodwill to join in the search for peace. Christians, whose Master has called us to be peacemakers, can hardly afford to ignore this crucial task. No one but a Christian can know the full scope of peace referred to in the Bible. But what better way for us to bear witness to that peace than by taking the lead in being peacemakers?

Dag Hammarskjold was secretary general of the United Nations from 1953 until his death in 1961—a tense period in world history. He was a man of deep Christian faith. The record of his spiritual pilgrimage came to light after his death and has been published in English under the title *Markings.* Hammarskjold was a man who had found the peace that passes understanding in his own life. He also was a peacemaker in every sense of the word. He found no contradiction between inner peace and outward efforts at peacemaking. As an individual and as a diplomat, he followed the way of the cross. He died while on a dangerous mission for the cause of peace.

Not every Christian can be a peacemaker on the level of this man, but each Christian has many opportunities to be a peacemaker. Keep in mind the total scope of the biblical view of peace: *Shalom* is more than the absence of war; it is the positive wholeness of man in harmony with God, others, and creation. As Jack Stotts wisely notes:

Peacemaking is not an intermittent task, provoked by the outbreak of armed conflict. It is an ongoing responsibility, requiring diligent activity toward the reconstitution of human life on all levels, from the individual through the institutional, and in all spheres, from the local through the international arenas of existence. [7]

Summary

1. *Shalom* is the key to the meaning of peace in the Bible. It refers to the ideal well-being of man in proper harmony with God, his fellow man, and all of God's creation.

2. God himself is the source and giver of peace. There is no contradiction between trusting God for peace and working with God toward peace.

3. God offers sinners a new state of peace with God through Jesus Christ. This inner peace is not dependent on peaceful circumstances but on doing the will of God.

4. God's purpose of peace includes peace among those who have been brought to God in Christ. The practice of this peace calls for the exercise of Christian love toward brothers in Christ.

5. Christians are called to live at peace, to pray for peace, and to be peacemakers in the world. We are called to be peacemakers at every level of society and in every way possible.

[1] Jack L. Stotts, *Shalom: The Search for a Peaceable City* (Nashville: Abingdon Press, 1973), pp. 112-13.

[2] David A. Redding, "Are Christians Stumbling Over Themselves?" *Christianity Today,* 19 Jan. 1968, p. 14.

[3] W. E. Sangster, "Can We Get 'Peace of Mind'?" *Christianity Today,* 29 Oct. 1956, p. 7.

[4] *Ibid.,* p. 5.

[5] Gordon C. Hunter, *When the Walls Come Tumblin' Down* (Waco: Word Books, 1970), p. 36.

[6] Douglas J. Harris, *The Biblical Concept of Peace Shalom* (Grand Rapids: Baker Book House, 1970), p. 60.

[7] *Op. cit.,* p. 202.